Cyril Cusack's
The Humour Is On Me

Cyril Cusack's
The Humour Is On Me

Compiled by Cyril Cusack
Illustrations by Rowel Friers

Appletree Press
Belfast

First published in Northern Ireland by
The Appletree Press Ltd
7 James Street South
Belfast BT2 8DL
1980

ISBN 0 904651 65 7

Copyright © Appletree Press Ltd 1980

All royalties to the Simon Community, Ireland

Cover photograph by Johnny Morris
Designed by Martin Storie. Edited by Peter Carr
James Galway appears by kind permission of Elm Tree Press

Printed by A. Wheaton & Co. Ltd., Exeter

CONTENTS

Foreword by Cyril Cusack   7

FORWARD!

To be serious: should one be anything but deadly serious about a matter so delicate as the 'Irish sense of humour', not to speak of the unspeakable, the less than delicate 'Irish joke'—believed by the patriot few to be the latest lethal invention of the traditional enemy?

Once, for consideration by an Irish Jesuit, rather cynically I ventured the distinction that, whereas wit, of that special brand precious and peculiar to the Irish intelligence, is largely motivated by malice, humour—less native?—may be charged with the spirit of charity. My Jesuit said that most certainly he would consider it!

I had come to wonder—before attempting to winkle out these few jewels of joy—whether the 'Irish sense of humour' was no more than a happy hallucination or a fake pearl such as Broadbent of Bernard Shaw's 'John Bull's Other Island' might cast to the deriding natives. Of course, I am proven wrong. What is to be seen here—with that infamous 'broken mirror' held up, trembling, to Irish good-nature—is a somewhat enigmatic face, creased, as the winds blow, with a whole series of changing expressions; what transpires is at least a *sense* of an 'Irish sense of humour'.

From where I write (surrounded by a motley array of smiles captured—on paper!—from poets, sportsmen, actors, politicians, bravely seeking out a way of life through laughter) here in this small Westmeath village, amidst the hush of rain and a rush of chattering rooks, I hear the high-pitched, almost whinneying laugh of a farmer gamely saving hay from the grey, wet summer. Where is the source of that bright laugh, the secret of his humour—the mystery? Does it lie somewhere between the sad comicality of human endeavour in collision with the unexpected and even, at times, the expected, and ironic acceptance of man's frailty at odds with his universe and his gods? Perhaps that is it and this is best.

I do not expect the reader's face to break easily into a glorious galaxy of grins and giggles, and if this selection fails to evoke hilarious reaction, or indeed nothing more than a gentle amusement, why should we be displeased! It may provide an insight into the person behind the anecdote, even a revelation of what so many different people see as being funny and, from that, perhaps a better understanding of the human predicament.

I think it is an acceptable cliche that, given a sense of humour, man may grapple more confidently with the moods and tenses of life and even—in Irish circles, at any rate (*vide* James Galway)—that other joker, death.

So, from this bizarre assemblage, this veritable cross-section of the Irish people from all four quarters of the country, North, South, East and West, from male and female, religious, non-religious, comes the humour of Ireland—many faces of the laughing god. It comes from all angles, reaching from the apocryphal 'bull' and gentle reminiscence, through devastated dignity and slapstick, down to the humbling tumble of the clown.

Since the god makes so many funny faces, it would be invidious to try to situate 'Irish humour' within the confine of a narrow national context or, still more narrowly, erecting superfluous borders, to departmentalise it into areas. Humour is individual and idiosyncratic as well as being circumstantial, and, in its myriad manifestations, is well beyond the reach of that imperious 'final analysis' so frequently recognizable as the ultimate deception.

The common factor running through this slender but select compendium is human vulnerability; the more human and vulnerable, then, you might say, the more distinctively Irish—bringing it dangerously into line with the 'Irish joke'.

I have my favourites, of course. Perhaps because, I play clerical roles, amongst others, I lean more towards the ecumenical anecdote. The liberated literary personage might take a further liberty with the old proprieties and, while that part of me still puritan may rebel against the ruderies and vulgarisms of the day, who

9

dare banish Rabelais from the Irish scene! I am relieved at the absence of that maelstrom of malice and Old Testament retribution erupting into vindictiveness: your Punch and Judy kind of humour. Rather let this be a salutary stroll along bypaths and alleyways, in and out of mazes maybe, with some amusement, even wonderment, at antics and experiences not too dissimilar from our own, to learn from others something of ourselves.

Most anecdotes are left as written. One, for instance, remains in a state of *non*-punctuation, not for exposure to the critic but rather to retain the quality of the personality—*a la* autobiography of Trader Horne, a best-seller of the long ago. To Forsyth, as visitor to our shores nuptually Hibernicised, I give pride of place. The native, of course, as is 'the custom of the country' (a quip current in Boucicault farce with the old Irish touring company) will 'catch-as-catch-can'. And so, from the highways and byways, let the good and holy clowns march bravely in, satisfied to sit at table—the first all-Ireland gathering of its kind!

We may be moved to merriment—or otherwise!—from having met some of these contributors, from having seen others on television, or even from having been 'informed' of others out of the mouth of gossip. Idiosyncracies of dialect would fire the telling of a tale. Nevertheless, even without the aid of such contacts, the reader is invited to join in with his contribution, as a good audience-member, to this family circle.

And for good measure and to indicate that we can put prejudice aside, happily I close 'Spike' Milligan's vintage example of the 'Irish joke'. (See page 67)

Finally, pity the man who cannot shed a tear; more to be pitied is he who cannot cast the shadow of a smile.

Cyril Cusack
Castletowngeoghagan

Frederick Forsyth

NOVELIST

My first visit to Ireland took place two days before the end of 1973, when the lovely Irish girl I was engaged to proposed we visit the land of her fathers. After landing at Aldergrove we rented a car and set off through the Glens of Antrim, arriving in the smiling village of Ballycastle at around lunchtime. We duly installed ourselves in the one hotel that seemed to be open for lunch. The waitress approached. We were silently handed a menu comprising a 'Soup of the Day' and a choice of six main courses: roast pork, loin of veal, lamb cutlets, liver and bacon, gammon steak and boiled beef. The waitress hovered expectantly.

'Soup, dear?'

'Yes.'

'Two soups,' said the waitress and jotted it down. We were slowly perusing the main courses when an uncompromising Antrim accent cut through our thoughts: 'It's all off,' she said, looking down at us expressionlessly.

'All off?' I asked faintly.

'Except the lamb cutlets.'

'We'll take them!'

'...and there's only one.'

'What else is there?'

'I don't know...'

I did the chivalrous thing: Carrie had the cutlets and after an interval of suspense I was served with two fried eggs and a rind of bacon.

Denise Webster

AUTHOR

I was driving from our hotel in Frankfurt to the Book Fair when, without warning, right in the middle of the rush-hour traffic, the car stopped dead. Try as I would I could't get it to budge.

As my husband and I looked blankly at each other a kindly German pulled in and indicated that he would tow us to a nearby garage. We thanked him as best we could and he left us on the forecourt.

As my husband had an important appointment he had to leave me—with a phrase book—to sort things out. Just then I noticed that the petrol cap was missing. As things had quietened somewhat I was able to corner the attendant long enough to indicate with gestures that the cap had been removed during the night—perhaps something nasty had been put in the tank. For a while he looked very puzzled then recognition lit his face: we understood one another. With a great beaming smile he took me by the elbow—and led me to the ladies toilet!

Constantine Fitzgibbon
AUTHOR AND BIOGRAPHER

In the summer of 1966 I rented a house on the shore of the still oil-less Bantry Bay. Since I was to have a serious eye operation that winter, I indulged myself by buying the best gramophone available—a Leek by name—and a number of records. The Leek arrived unassembled and without a box. A friend from Dublin who understands such matters came down and assembled it. He told me that it must immediately be encased since even turf smoke from the fire would affect its superlative mechanism.

I therefore ordered a simple box from a carpenter in Bantry called Mr O'Sullivan—as are most of that pleasant port's inhabitants. I sat back and waited. At this point it must be explained that like virtually all educated Irishmen of my generation my 'accent' is—to any but a trained ear—undistinguishable from that of an educated Englishman. Further, I then held Irish and American passports. In 1940 I had decided that the policy of neutrality pursued by my two countries was neither honourable nor wise, and like 160,000 other Irishmen, I joined the British forces, in my case the Irish guards. As a recruit at the Guards' Depot, Caterham, I learned much for which I have had little use since. Above all I learned a comprehensive vocabulary of obscenities; the complex mixture of blasphemy and scatology that was hurled at us with relish by our skilled NCOs.

One night in the midst of dinner, there was a ring at the front door. It was—to my considerable astonishment—

Mr O'Sullivan and a friend with the box. Unsteadily, he carried the thing through the heavy rain into the drawing room. To my even greater surprise it fitted the Leek to perfection. I paid them, gave them the statutory drink, watched them totter towards their van and returned to my now cold meal.

Almost at once I heard the unmistakable noise of car wheels revolving, but not progressing, on wet grass. I hastened out, with torch, to help. It was of no avail, we could not shoulder the van out of the grass, the incline was too steep. Within minutes its wheels were six inches deep and kicking out earth like four small dredgers. The rain poured upon us.

'Which of you is the less drunk?' I asked.

'I am,' said Mr O'Sullivan's friend.

'You will drive and O'Sullivan and I will push, you blithering idiots.'

I could not stop. Buried in my unconscious for some 26 years, the torrent of Caterham vernacular roared forth. The effect was stunning, at any rate it stunned me. To the background of this stream of abuse Mr O'Sullivan and I heaved, the soberer one drove, and the van was returned to the road. Only then did I fall silent. As they prepared to drive off, I heard one remark to the other: 'Didn't I tell ya? When he forgets himself he talks like a normal man.'

Barry White

JOURNALIST

My family has a long history of embarrassing moments, going back to the day when my brother ended a French oral examination with a grand flourish and an 'Au revoir, Monsieur' and stepped smartly into the wall. Journalistically, I put my foot in it in October 1968 when I had the choice of spending a quiet Saturday afternoon at home or driving up to Derry to see what all this civil rights fuss was about and settled for my armchair.

But I topped the lot this winter, on a skiing holiday in Bulgaria. I attempted to recapture my youth on the top slopes and ended up with an inside-out knee. Skiing was out so I decided to take the midnight express to Istanbul—from nearby Plovdiv—returning the following night. The bus and train times had been carefully co-ordinated so as to leave me three hours to limp about Plovdiv. I surveyed the points of interest and returned to the railway station where I used my most expressive sign language to confirm that the Istanbul train was due on platform four.

I was out on the track—they don't go in for platforms in Plovdiv—with twenty minutes to spare. 'Four?' I fingered to the station staff: they shook their heads in agre^ment. All was well. There was even an automatic train indicator which clicked round to a reassuring 'Istanbul Express 10.25'. It was hot so I doused myself at the fountain and began to wonder how would I survive the journey without liquids. I wondered even harder when a big train drew up two platforms away. A succession of people raced out and spent a good five minutes filling up every available container. They left in a blaze of lights, but still platform four was empty. The train must be late. The sign indicating the next train caught my eye; it changed to something indecipherable in Cyrillic.

I went back to the station. The next train would be tomorrow evening. I spent the night in a hotel and caught the first bus back, arriving just in time to meet the first skiers on their way to the slopes. 'How had I found Istanbul?'

'I didn't like it', I replied.

John McGuffin

AUTHOR

I very rarely have embarrassing moments. This I
ascribe to my savoir faire, charm and tact. My wife and
friends have been known to ascribe it to pig ignorance
and a thick skin—but I have learned to live with
jealousy.

On reflection—thank you, darling—perhaps there
are one or two isolated incidents. On the *Peoples'
Democracy* 'Long March' from Belfast to Dublin at
Easter in 1969, we made speeches at every town and
Balbriggan. As ritual demanded, we set up our loud-
speakers in the village square. The sensible marchers,
who had heard it all before, retreated to the pubs
and left me to the 60 or so locals. I stood halfway
up a flight of steps and cleared my throat: 'People of
Dundalk . . .'

I recall being invited to a party which was attended by
several MPs. I remember I had been asked there solely
because I had just published a book. The hostess and a
young man stood by the buffet, I approached her to pay
my respects: 'Mrs Aaaaah,' I prattled gaily, 'nice of
your son and you to invite me.' She glanced icily
towards a point somewhere just above my right
shoulder: 'Actually, Paul's my husband, Mr Emm
ehhh.' Strange to say I have not been invited back.

Finally, I should like to relate the tale of a young man
from West Belfast who was sent out to paint wall
slogans warning informers to keep their mouths shut.

19

The young man completed his mission and returned to bed. The following day the residents of Andersonstown's Bignian Drive woke to view the slogan: 'Trouts Beware.'

The following evening some wag painted beneath it: 'Up the Aquarian Revolution.'

Alex 'Hurricane' Higgins

SNOOKER PLAYER

On sunny afternoon my wife and I went for a drive through Lancashire's lush and pleasant countryside. We had clear roads, blue skies, fresh air—apart from the bluebottles and horseflies it was paradise. After a few miles we came to a main road. There was a yellow Fiat parked on the left kerb; as my wife overtook it, two cars screamed out from a side road—we only just avoided them.

We parked in the nearest lay-by to have a cigarette and recover. My wife decided she'd had enough so I took the wheel and we headed back through the countryside. A GPO van approached us round a left-hand bend. Easy does it, I thought, and went for the brake, only to merrily plant my foot on the accelerator. We surged into the hedge. You might describe the effect as shattering. We emerged unharmed in a cloud of gnats and horseflies. The joys of country motoring—gimme the smog!

Theodora Fitzgibbon

AUTHOR

Driving from Cork to Dublin on one of those rare, balmy summer days, we stopped at the hotel at Cahir for refreshments. Some wanted beer, others tea: we ordered two beers, a pot of ordinary Indian tea and a pot of China tea from the somewhat nervous looking girl.

'It's ridiculous to expect China tea in the country,' I said. 'We'll be here for hours, gasping.'

Sure enough we waited and waited. The girl returned looking like a frightened heifer at a fair.

'It's about the tea,' she said.

I passed my partner an I-told-you-so glance.

'We've China tea all right, but no Indian, only ordinary Irish.'

My partner had the decency not to respond.

Paddy Hopkirk

RALLY-DRIVER AND ENTREPRENEUR

In the early days of my rallying career I was leading in a rally which had one of its special stages on a squiggly tarmac road near Fivemiletown. I had been pushing my luck all day. In the evening the inevitable happened: I overdid it on one of those semi-spherical humpback bridges; my mini came down on its nose and rolled end over end. However, thanks to roll-over bars, seat belts and crash helmets, my co-driver and I emerged with nothing hurt except pride.

We spent the night in the village inn. When I awoke, black and blue, on Sunday morning, I decided maybe I should go to church and give thanks for being alive.

The local church was very primitive: all the men were seated on the one side and all the women on the other. As for the minister—well! To call him 19th century is to absurdly understate him, the man was from another era! After he had delivered a sermon of rolling Dickensian hell-fire, the time for collection came. To my astonishment, he decended from the pulpit, plate in hand, and began to march among the pews. He stopped in front of his first parishioners:

'Mrs Casey, five shillin's! Mr Beggs, two and sex!'

He approached my row, I scoured my pockets. I had sixpence. He stopped in front of me. Purple with embarrassment I edged the small coin onto his plate. Trembling, I looked up and met his eyes. A sympathetic expression flitted across his face. He called, 'Stranger, sexpence!' and passed on.

Jack McBride

AUTHOR

Several years ago I served on a small oil tanker. One
November we were docked in Belfast beside a similar
French boat when orders came aboard to load for
Iceland. As we were in port we took full advantage of
the opportunity to equip ourselves for the rigours of the
Icelandic winter: we brought fleecy duffle coats, thick
seaboot socks, elbow length gauntlets and 'Dr Who'
type scarves topped by woollen hats of many shapes
and colours.

Thus fortified, we left Belfast and boldly set out for
the land of the glacier. The French tanker received
similar instructions: bragging that they would be there
before us, they set out slightly earlier that morning.

After several days we saw the tips of the snow-clad
mountains of the island's interior. It wasn't long before
we entered the fiord at whose head was Reykjavik, the
principal city. From my station deep in the ship's
bowels I imagined us battling up the fiord. Apparently
a crowd of dockers and sightseers had gathered on the
quayside to see who would arrive first. Encased in our
mountains of knitwear, we emerged: to find Reykjavik
no cooler than a mild March morning!

'It's the Irish,' some bright spark crowed.

Mary Robinson

SENATOR

Election campaigns are tough on the children of a candidate, particularly if she is their mother. It is true that there are compensations by way of shiny badges to swap at school, and a distinguished vocabulary full of words such as 'constituency' and 'advice clinic'. But still: bedtime stories are rushed, meals missed and parents look harassed and exhausted.

Shortly after the local elections in June 1979 the message was brought home to me in no uncertain terms. I was opening the post at breakfast when a letter bearing a Labour Party logo emerged.

'Mum, is that from the Labour Party?' asked five-year-old William.

'That's right dear', I replied abstractedly, only to receive a fierce rejoinder: 'But mum, I thought the Labour Party was over!'

Jim Sim

BANKER

On a two day business trip to Dublin I was joined by my
wife and her sister: they to weary themselves shopping,
I to refresh myself at the fountain called Head Office.
Anxious to discover the crock of gold at the end of the
rainbow (as indicated by the downcurve of our progress
graph) the chairman invited me to stay a third day. The
ladies however could not delay their return. They took
the car and permitted me the comfort of the train. After
seeing them off, I called into reception to change my
'suite'—adjoining bedrooms with common bathroom/
toilet—for a 'single'. Knowing the chairman would be
reluctant to end the fun early I indicated my likely take
up time as midnight plus: then promptly left for the
meeting.

Returning at 1.00 am I was informed that I was to
occupy the same room. It was not until I had undressed
that I discovered my pyjamas had gone—in fact everything that I had brought with me was missing. A
hurried phone call to Peter the nightman—hurried on
my part leisurely on his—revealed that my effects had
been treated as 'forgotten baggage'. He assured me that
he would rescue it in the morning. Further, he promised—on the lives of saints too numerous to mention—
that he would wake me in time to catch the 8.00 am train.
Thus comforted, I joined the moderns and slept in the
nude.

Sure enough, my parcelled belongings were returned
next morning together with profuse explanation and

apology. Early morning is not my best time but I managed to enquire the hour. Midday! Shriek!

Tearing apart the parcel I grabbed my shaving kit and hit the bathroom fast. Panting heavily, I clicked the door closed. Suddenly there was a shrill scream. An enthroned female leapt up and promptly sprawled full-length on the floor. My innocent effort to assist her to the vertical created pandimonium: 'Aaah! Aaah! Eddie! *HELP!*' Full of the honeymooning husband's protective aggression Eddie burst from the adjoining room . . .

How I avoided a mauling is another story.

Louis le Brocquy

ARTIST

It is said that a painter tends to paint his own image in everything. I suppose that is natural enough, since his subject—be it a tree, a sky, or another human being—is inevitably reflected onto his canvas from somewhere within his own head. Try as we may, it seems we are condemned to paint our own insides and, more alarming, our insides may be recognised on sight.

Mine were spotted early. In 1947 the Gimpel Gallery in London gave me my first one-man show. At that time I was passionately interested in the Travelling People, the Irish 'Tinkers', and most of my pictures were images of these wild, wandering families, whose isolated and unpredictable existence seemed to parallel the quiet individualism of the artist.

Imagine then my pleasure on opening day when a small grey lady approached me, declaring: 'You are the artist, I know it. I recognised you at once from your painting.' Had she perceived in me something of what Yeats described as 'the swift, indifferent man'? I said as much.

'Ah, no,' she replied earnestly, 'it wasn't the Tinkers. It was that over there—the white cow.'

George Simms

FORMERLY CHURCH OF IRELAND ARCHBISHOP OF ARMAGH AND PRIMATE OF ALL-IRELAND

As the newly appointed dean of a cathedral in a busy city my first move was to meet a few of my parishioners.

I began by knocking on the door of a long established resident in the parish. She squinted at me from the doorstep. She saw the bicycle and, I suppose, my youthfulness. I hoped she did not perceive the rawness that accompanied my immaturity. I was admitted.

We opened with the usual weather-jottings and neighbourhood musings. The flow of talk was sluggish. There was a stickiness. My shyness did not help. My general remarks—I felt forced to repeat them for clearer reception—sounded flat and particularly banal. I skirmished round some subjects of human interest but never a gleam of the spiritual shone through.

Nonetheless she seemed to be warming to me; she seemed to appreciate the call and the contact. At this point I had the curious sensation that she was beginning to feel sorry for me. She kept referring to my youthfulness and how difficult it must be working at the cathedral in these changed times. As we drank I reflected on her grasp of, and sympathy for, my problems. I rose to go. It takes time to catch another's wave-length.

We were in the hall. The door was open. She turned to me and in a loud voice that was surely heard over the hedge: 'Good luck! I've heard about your new dean but I'm sure he'll come round given time.'

Maurice Craig
ARCHITECTURAL HISTORIAN

I recall travelling Connaught with Louis McNiece several years ago. We came across a level-crossing, the gate of which was neither open nor shut. The keeper sat on a stile relishing a cigarette. When we approached he greeted us cordially. In answer to our query he told us that he was half-expecting a train.

Is this a 'bull'? I think it is a kind of 'counter-bull'. His remark was not entirely without merit, for though it was not entirely rational it had at least the appearance of logicality. The converse is the remark which is illogical in form but forcibly clear in meaning, the force deriving from the intermediate steps being unexpressed. A short while ago at a time of great postal uncertainty I only just stopped myself from writing: 'Let me know if you do not get this letter.' I wonder how many got away.

Alf MacLochlainn
LIBRARIAN AND WRITER

Most of the few people who know me probably think of me (when they think of me at all) as a librarian. Drawing myself up to my full height, however, I wish to state that I am also a writer. The late Myles na Gopaleen once quoted from a piece I had written, prefacing his remarks with an attribution to 'the writer Alf MacLochlainn'.

I had just read an attempt by a Japanese publisher to promote sales of a work on judo. His prospectus included such gems as: 'You may throw him on his rear by wrenching your body, so to speak, in a wringing way . . .' My piece was a simple plea to writers of English never to try to write in Japanese.

Shortly before the piece appeared in 'Hibernia', Myles and I were chatting about Denis Johnston's *Nine Rivers from Jordan,* then newly published. He was particularly amused by Johnston's illustration of journalist's telegraphese. A journalist lost in the fleshpots of the Middle East received a cable from his editor asking tersely, *'Why unnews?'* To this he had replied, *'Unnews goodnews.'* The editor's rejoinder, *'Unnews unjob'* elicited the economical resignation, *'Upshove job arsewards.'*

Having submitted the judo piece instead of my regular column of film criticism I departed for the smoke of London. To my surprise I received a telegram from *Hibernia:* 'Unfilm copy', it ran. I replied: 'Ah-so.' I think Myles would have liked that.

Dana

SINGER

I was doing a European concert tour in 1971: Amsterdam, Paris, Berlin, each night we were in a different country. The mild 'flu I had at the beginning of the tour got worse as the tour progressed. Exhausted, and not feeling at all well, I left Berlin for our next destination, which I had been told was Venice. We arrived late, and I went straight to bed.

Next morning I decided to do some sight-seeing. I went down to the hotel foyer and asked the porter where I might find the gondolas. The man seemed very amused. I asked if he spoke English. He replied that he did. So I again asked if he could please tell me how to get to the gondolas.

He returned a bemused, somewhat sympathetic smile. Befuddled though I was, it dawned on me that one of us was under a very big misapprehension.

'Where am I?' I asked.

'Vienna!'

TH – C

Charlie Nash

BOXER

In the summer of 1976 Ray Ross and I were fighting separate bouts on the same night in London. When my fight finished I took a taxi to the Cafe Royale to watch Ray. As the first fight had lasted only two rounds Ray and his opponent had to take the ring earlier than expected. Though they spilled out of the dressing room in some confusion, they managed to climb into the ring with all the poise of title fighters.

Ray was introduced. He took off his gown and limbered up. The compere continued, 'In the blue corner we have Alan Richardson, British Featherweight champion.' The crowd cheered. Blissfully ignorant that he was wearing nothing but his boots and gumshield, Alan eased off his gown . . .

He went on to win.

Patrick Campbell

WRITER AND BROADCASTER

My 1000 word Monday-to-Friday *Irish Times* column, 'An Irishman's Diary', was giving me regular night mares. After an hour or so's groaning and thrashing, I would wake up at 4 o'clock in the morning believing I had forgotten or been unable to write my contribution to the paper the previous day. It was my own fault. I had no system for writing the column. No note-book, no back-up of possible ideas for development, no connection with the News Room. I just set off on my bicycle about 10 o'clock every morning, hoping that something would happen.

Throughout this daily tour I was chilled and haunted by an observation made by Robert Maire Smyllie, my 18-stone editor, concerning a certain unfortunate scratching for 'crumbs of news on an unforgiving tar-macadam road . . .'. It was this veiled jab that involved me in the infamous 'Huguenot Embroglio'. A clergyman wrote to me to call my attention to 'the ruinous condition of Dublin's historic Huguenot cottages. 'I may add,' he concluded, that the Huguenots were, of course, Protestant,' regarding this, obviously, as a *bonne bouche* for *The Irish Times*. Determined to excell myself, I got on my bike and rode.

I found the mouldering cottages and rejected them on sight as a Diary subject. All they were doing was falling down. It was at this moment the Rhinocerous Crone tottered out of a black doorway carrying a naked baby, which appeared, at the very least, to have measles

from head to toe. The old woman had a huge lump in the middle of her forehead which named her for me forever. A moment later I was surrounded by three derelict men and a youngish woman in rags carrying two more spotted babies. They bustled me indoors, making pleas for money, food and clothes that seemed to have been bottled up inside them for years. They all lived in a ground-floor room which was held together by four iron tie-bars ranged about 4-feet above the floor. Serving as wardrobes, these were draped with rags, making it almost impossible to move around except by stepping high.

After an hour in their company I went back to the office and wrote a thundering denunciation of a government which could permit human degradation on this Belsen level to exist in the midst of our fair city. .

When the column appeared the following day I was widely accused of having made it up. It died without further comment.

Two weeks later Mr Smyllie sent for me. 'Mr Campbell,' he said, 'you've got your shuddering Huguenots back to front.' 'Shuddering' was his favourite epithet, covering all errors in taste, and in this case, fact. 'They have a combined income,' Mr Smyllie said, 'of approximately £42 a week, provided by pensions, contributions from Liverpool and similar emoluments. Every penny of it has gone on drink and dogs by 11 o'clock on Saturday night.

With care he lit his curved flowerpot pipe. 'Mr de Valera himself took me to task, touching weightily on Protestant propaganda. I wrote him with moderate apologies. He did not reply, so the matter is closed. He rose to his awesome full extent. 'You would do well to leave the shuddering reporting to others.'

I have taken that wise advice ever since.

Jeremy Addis

PUBLISHER

Messing about in boats was a simple pleasure I was reluctant to give up when I moved to London. I thought I had the problem licked when I discovered my girl-friend—now wife—lived on a houseboat on the Thames. One morning I turned up at the boat with a battered sailing dinghy and an overgrown pooch called Roper, intent on introducing my intended to the joys of sailing.

The adventure was a disaster. A fresh breeze eddied merrily round the wharfs and warehouses: powering us, becalming us, then pouncing from another quarter to gybe us all standing. Deirdre soon learned that survival demanded agility. Roper knew something was expected of him but never quite discovered what and within fifteen minutes he had succeeded in entangling himself in every rope in the boat.

While Roper did a thorough job of making the dinghy completely unnavigable the tide carried us down upon the Albert Bridge. Underneath it there are a series of a dozen or so girders specially constructed to be just slightly less tall than our mast so that every time we passed one we shipped a generous dollop of Thames. That was it. Enough! I struck for the shore.

The ebb was now in full rip and we were unable to avoid smashing into the bows of the big launch moored just below the pier. My little tub played havoc with its ornate gilt scrollwork. As there was nothing to get a grip on we scraped and grazed our way down the whole length of the boat. We finally fetched up just below it. A

38

taciturn longshoreman took our rope.

'I'm afraid we've spoiled your launch's paintwork,' I ventured, 'perhaps I ought to have a word with the owner?'

'You can try,' he replied, 'she lives up the road there; you've sliced up the Royal Barge.'

Sile de Valera
TD AND EUROPEAN MP

June 1977 and the day of the General Election. Ten minutes before the booths closed an old man arrived in the company of an Airedale dog—both of them festooned in opposition regalia. In the unlikely prospect of a last minute conversion my assistant offered him some Fianna Fail propaganda—he refused this in no uncertain terms.

When the pair re-emerged the Airdale and another dog began fighting: it took two men to separate them. In the confusion I found myself shoulder to shoulder with my opposition. 'I know things aren't going well for us, Sile,' he whispered, 'but this dogfight goes to Fine Gael.'

Lord Longford
AUTHOR AND PUBLISHER

I suppose nearly everyone has at least one embarrassing moment etched into their memory forever; I have a vast and nigh innumerable catalogue.

On one occasion, while staying with my aunt, Lady Dunsany, at Dunsany Castle, I mistook her bedroom, for my own. I am alleged to have climbed into her nightdress and then into her bed having already mistaken her eye lotion for my nightly medicine.

As by now you will have gathered, I don't do these things by halves. At the Oxford Point-to-Point horse

race, I excelled myself by colliding with the first fence. Though the crash was emphatic, I emerged losing only my crash helmet, and doggedly carried on. I was in the process of thanking my lucky stars when I promptly crashed into another. Mildly concussed, I started riding the wrong way round the course, and in a scene reminiscent of the medieval joust nearly unhorsed the winner.

Needless to say, when the incident is mentioned, I protest to remember nothing.

Frank Carson
COMEDIAN

My dad loved to accompany me to a show and would be very proud when I introduced him as my father. One one such occasion I was performing in Bangor, a seaside resort in County Down. At Holywood, some six or seven miles from Belfast, a large city dump has been reclaimed and an oil refinery built on the site. Over 300 million tons of concrete were used in its construction. We passed large storage tanks and long flues expelling excess gas in fiery fountains. 'That place is a tribute to man's ingenuity,' I remarked. Father looked out at the conglomerate of smoke and steel and said: 'I could have told them there was oil there 40 years ago!'

Terry de Winne

MANAGER OF THE ULSTER HALL, BELFAST

Saturday evenings, for me, are usually a restful time: time to pile the logs on the fire, put the feet up and relax. I am a lucky man really: although most of the activity of the Ulster Hall and the Group Theatre takes place during the evenings, I have an excellent back-up team who ably deal with most emergencies.

There are exceptions. One occurred on an evening such as I have described. At half past ten the phone rang. A hassle with a promoter was in full swing—he said that I had said that he could carry on till 1 am on Sunday. The caretaker, being in full possession of both the facts and his faculties, told him that there was no way that this punk—or any other—concert would continue after midnight. I was needed to lay down the law.

Now, my office is a converted cloakroom which one enters via the outer door of the ladies' toilets. My innocent progress has raised many an eyebrow in its time and this evening was no exception: I entered with the promoter. Fifteen minutes later, all was under control. He left and I locked up behind him.

On emergence I almost collided with a spectacular apparition. Her hair was streaked with green and silver, her pallid complexion broken by a gash of heavy black eye make-up and lip-stick that would have delighted a pillar-box painter. She looked me up and down: 'What're *you* doin' comin' outa the ladies?'

Alas, to my everlasting shame, I did not have the wit to ask her what she was doing going in!

Henry Kelly

JOURNALIST AND AUTHOR

At the bottom of Belfast's Newtownards Road is the Catholic enclave of the Short Strand. It is surrounded by Protestant houses and people. It in turn envelops Austin Street, a tiny Protestant terrace. This area is what was known as a flash-point area: if there was to be trouble in East Belfast it was liable to begin thereabouts.

In June and July 1970 the city was torn by street rioting. It was vicious, sectarian and bloody dangerous. It was not safe to be on the streets out of your own area. It was worthwhile for the press to hunt in packs. Now when things got tough we reporters could crouch behind walls or hide behind army vehicles but cameramen could afford no such luxury. No-one has yet invented a successful system for taking photographs round corners. The men with the cameras suffered a lot: they had to get close and when they got too close a mob would take its wrath out on them; missiles meant for policemen and soldiers would shower on our colleagues. Often their bravery was doubly useful: they got brilliant pictures by taking risks and they would come back to where we writers crouched and give us extra lines for our stories.

Day-time rioting was not exactly unknown in East Belfast during those months. From a window in Austin Street—and I always checked it as I moved gingerly up the Newtownards Road behind a line of soldiers—a Union Jack, and later an Ulster flag, flew defiantly. Whether there was more than one Protestant family I never found out, anyway, the women there made up in noise what they lacked in numbers. The East Belfast lady has in many cases learned how to speak by trying to talk louder than the sound of steel riveting from the nearby shipyards. Often too the voice and accent combine to remind one of nothing so much as the sound of metal on metal. One of the ladies of Austin Street was fearless; her specialty was anti-Popish slogans directed at pressmen.

One sunny afternoon, as we advanced slowly into a hail of missiles—behind two lines of soldiers and a bevvy of policemen—Mrs Austin Street advanced with us, umbrella at the ready in case of emergency or a pressman.

She picked her target and moved in. First, she hit the television cameraman over the back but since he was wearing a hugh anorak and a bullet-proof vest she damn near broke the umbrella. He politely told her to go away. She hit him across the ankles.

She persisted but the cameraman kept filming. No matter. Mrs Austin Street would still be able to tell the girls that she'd 'given them lying pressmen a piece of her mind'.

Eventually there came a lull in the riot: the cameraman laid down his heavy burden on the ground but his shadowing burden remained at his elbow, umbrella at the ready. It looked like we were in for a re-run; faithful to a colleague to the last, the rest of us stood around trying to look like a tour-bus load of evangelists. In exasperation the cameraman looked her in the eye: 'Look, missus, I don't care who you are or who anybody here is. I'm just doing my job, OK? I'm just taking pictures, you know. Photos for TV, OK? I'm just taking photographs. All right?'

Mrs Austin Street was never at a loss for words.

'That might be so, Mister Smart Alick,' she said with the softness of a girder going through a mangle, 'but,'—and she leaned forward, umbrella held high in anticipation of her forthcoming triumph—'you're photographin' things that ain't happenin'.'

Tony O'Reilly

CHAIRMAN OF THE HEINZ CORPORATION

In 1969, seven years after my last game of rugby for Ireland, to my consternation I was asked to play on the wing against England at Twickenham. This presented me with the not insignificant problem of reaching match fitness and at the same time meeting my extensive business obligations. The commonsense, if ostentatious, consequence was that I was chauffuered to and from practices in a company limousine, which allowed me to work undisturbed in the back seat.

So the trudge to fitness began. Fortunately, such fitness as I did attain was never seriously put to the test. I record this with relief. As a winger playing in a long tradition of not passing the ball, I had precious little to do for most of the game. However, just before the final whistle I found myself reduced to an act of foolhardy bravery. A long English footrush was terminated when—quite out of character—I dived at the feet of the England pack. As I was emerging from momentary unconsciousness I heard a loud and, let me confess, Irish voice shout from the popular terrace '. . . and kick his bloody chauffeur while you're at it!'

Donal Foley

COLUMNIST 'IRISH TIMES'

I remember once I had the task of writing a series of articles on Lady Norah Docker, at that stage one of the more flamboyant members of her class. Each night we would go to one of her places of relaxation—like a restaurant or cinema. This particular night we decided to try the latter. Lady Docker's maid rang up the Haymarket Cinema to book seats and advise them of our arrival. The film was *Dracula,* and she had already seen it three times.

We were driven to the cinema in a gold-plated Daimler (her pride and joy). When we arrived at the cinema we were greeted effusively by the manager. This was not all. He had put down a red carpet which ran from the car across the footpath up the steps and into the foyer. A crowd gathered, people clapped—what do you do?—I acknowledged the applause.

We were shown the two best seats in the cinema. Lady Docker's particular joy was to witness Dracula performing the blood sucking ritual. The event approached. She began to get excited. Finally, she could not restrain herself and announced its imminence to me in a confidential stage whisper which was probably heard in Picadilly. The people around and behind us began to hiss 'Sssh. Sssh.' Lady Docker hissed back twice as loud, 'I won't Sssh!'

The manager heard the commotion and came to investigate. He promptly asked us both to leave. And this time there was no red carpet!

John Pepper

AUTHOR AND HUMORIST

I sat down after addressing and audience of women.

'Thank you,' said the chairwoman confidentially, '. . . much better than the clever speakers we usually have.'

Similarly I have yet to think of a response to the request made to me during a signing session for one of my books in a Co. Down bookseller's.

A well-dressed little woman came up to me, said, 'Could you autograph this for me, please?' and reached me Willie John McBride's book of rugby reminiscences.

TH – D

Willie John McBride
IRISH AND BRITISH LIONS RUGBY PLAYER

We had been on tour in New Zealand for several weeks. One evening after a good win, I was interviewed on national radio. Towards the end of a rather jovial exchange the lady asked me what I most missed about home: 'Soda farls and potato bread,' I replied, tongue in cheek.

Two mornings later when I descended the hotel staircase I was confronted by a mountain of tattie-bread. My English, Scottish and Welsh team mates blocked my cowardly attempt to slink upstairs!

At the close of the tour, a Maori chief presented me with an elaborately carved 5'6" staff. We were in Los Angeles airport en route home. The connecting flight arrived. Staff in hand, I strode across the tarmac and was first up the steps of the plane. The hostess awaited. She knew the game was rugby. She made a brave attempt: 'Welcome on board sir, I'll put your rugby stick in the back.'

Sam Hanna Bell

WRITER AND BROADCASTER

My first broadcasting venture after the war involved reviving a series called 'Provincial Journey'. Pre-war this came from studios in Belfast. Now we were able to transmit direct from the countryside. Keen to take advantage of the new technology I chose a village in the west, interviewed speakers, singers and musicians, and wrote the linking script. I submitted my completed plan to J. R. Mageean, then BBC Northern Ireland drama producer.

He had been called away and it was several days before he saw it. I returned to find J. R. at his desk. I can best describe his expression as thunderstruck. It seemed as if he was endeavouring to overcome some emotional upset. I asked J. R. if he had read the script.

He nodded dumbly.

'I see you've engaged a bagpipe band.'

'Yes, J. R.'

'40 of them?'

'The locals think very highly of their band, J. R.'

'And booked a tenor.'

'He's good. I checked with Music Department.'

His hand trembled, his eyes rolled. It slowly became apparent I had not quite appreciated the technical problems involved. Unfortunately the point of no return had long passed.

Hearts in our boots we travelled west. After the first run-through in the village hall the sensitive business of co-ordinating pipes and tenor drove

J. R. to the bar. We were on our own. The programme engineer placed the tenor as close to the microphone as was possible. I organised a relay of local lads to hand-signal each other from the hall, down the corridor, round the corner and out into the main street where the band waited expectantly.

At the appointed moment singer and pipers got off to a boisterous if ragged start. It was the first time such a musical combination had been heard on the air and, as far as I am aware, the last.

Cecil Sheridan
ACTOR AND COMEDIAN

'Encore!'
'More!'
'More!'

Alas, the cheeres were not for me but Eddie Ferry, banjoist extraordinary. I was following Eddie with a parody act about a trembling hen-pecked husband, but believe me, on this occasion the trembling was for real: following him could be death.

Eddie was an old hand at milking an audience and finished his act with a medley of favourites. The whistling and enthusiastic foot stamping was deafening. Loath to let things die Eddie burst into another song, simultaneously signalling the stage manager for more time. The manager would have none of it and waved him off.

My music struck up through the bedlam. I took a deep breath and walked on. I was firmly planted centre-stage when Ferry—not yet gone—careered back on. The man was evidently in the throes of some sort of ecstatic oblivion.

'One fool at a time!' some wit shouted. Eddie passed out in my arms. I was mortified. 'Sing him a lullaby Cecil!'

Terence de Vere White

NOVELIST, BIOGRAPHER AND SHORT STORY WRITER

I recall with sentimental affection the day I learnt what were always called *the facts of life* from Ted Bailey, a school friend. We both went to a Dublin day-school, travelled there independently, and came home on the same train.

On the way back two girls (sisters) from Bailey's station used to join us in our carriage. The elder was Ted's age, thirteen, the younger, aged eleven, was mine

One afternoon Bailey and I were sitting in our second-class compartment when the girls went by, the elder with flushed cheek and averted head, the younger trotting obediently behind, obviously under a strict injunction 'not to look'. I had grown fond of the company of the two ladies, and their extraordinary behaviour upset me very much. I was quite angry with Bailey when, looking rather sheepish, he confessed that the sudden deterioration in our entente was due to something he had said that morning. I pressed him to tell me what he had said but could not get any good of him. He was clearly ashamed. The next day, as we approached the railway station, I asked him again.

'Oh, I said "f—k!" when I slipped getting into the train,' he said.

'Oh I see.'

'She'll cool down after a bit.'

'Why not say you're sorry?'

'No use. She's furious and says she won't come home with us *ever* again.'

'But why's she so cross?'

'Well, after all—you do know what it means don't you?'

'Oh, yes . . . of course.'

'Well, then . . . ?'

'But still, I don't see . . .'

'Do you know what it means?'

'Of course.'

'OK, then, what does it mean?'

'I can't put it into words, but I know what it means all right.'

'You're a liar.'

'What does it mean then, since you're so clever?'

He told me as we were passing under the shadow of the bridge. I recoiled.

'You're not trying to tell me Mr and Mrs de Valera do that!' I laughed contemptuously at the suggestion, but the more I thought about it, the more clearly I could see the awful possibility that there might after all be something in Bailey's theory. The appearance of the world began to change. I felt disappointed, cheated, sad. In one fell thrust, Bailey had shaken my faith in the republican principle and the entire adult world.

Mike Murphy

BROADCASTER

Shortly after beginning my first series of *The Likes of Mike,* I was enjoying a drink in my local when I saw this gent lumber in my direction. He tapped me on the shoulder.

'Ey,' he asked, 'd'you be on the telly do ye?'

I assented with a nod and a mutter.

'Well,' he said, 'you're f----n' brutal.'

This time I nodded and mumbled. He stared at me derisively.

'You t'ink I'm f----n' jokin' doncha—well I'm not.'

I assured him with a nod, a mumble and a grimace that I understood him as a man of serious bent.

By this time the whole pub was listening. He gave a grunt of satisfaction and walked away. I exhaled quietly and feelingly. Three steps away he remembered.

'An' anudder t'ing, the wife hates ye too!' A pause before the coup de grace. 'An' she knows f--k all!'

Mary Peters

OLYMPIC GOLD MEDALLIST

Shortly after Munich I was invited to open a shopping complex near Belfast. A great crowd of very enthusiastic fans turned out to give me a cheer. I was very proud. One elderly lady pushed her way to the front of the crowd and shouted: 'Hey, Mary, give us yer autograph for me grandson.'

'Certainly,' I said. 'Have you got his autograph book with you?'

For answer she shoved a dirty piece of paper at me and said: 'Oh no! I wouldn't carry it. Sure put it on this and he can copy it in when I get home.'

Uel Deane

NOMADIC TENOR

The large club in Tredeger, Land of Song, was filled to capacity. I had laid out my props, changed and was sitting in the dressing room waiting to meet the organist. He entered: an imposing figure in a scarlet dinner jacket who bore himself with an air of quiet superiority. I showed him the music and he flipped through each song with the confidence of a master. Now when this happens he can be very very good or very very bad. I like musicians who ask the odd question: problems solved in the dressing room can prevent an awful lot of embarrassment on stage. 'Do be careful about *On with the Motley*,' I explained, 'it starts off in E minor then goes into A minor and . . .'

'I don't play minors,' he said. I thought this was hilarious. 'I don't play bloody minors Bach.'

'Oh,' (going along with the joke) 'what do you play?'

'I play C, G, and B flat.'

'But my first number is in A.'

'Uh. Uh. Tonight it's in G.' Through the partition a thousand people were getting restless—he had to be kidding.

I bounced on; he sat morosely at the organ, holding down a strange chord. It was as if John Cage or Schonberg were having an off day. I can recognise defeat when it is staring me in the face: taking a totally ignored bow I walked off.

I was in the middle of packing when the concert secretary appeared.

'What's the matter Bach—voice blow up?'

'Your organist can't play.'

'What d'ya mean,' he snarled. 'Listen boyoo, every Sunday he plays the Dam Busters, booteeful it is, pulls the 'ouse down, and you have the bloody cheek to tell me he can't play! I think you'd better sod-off, boyoo.' I did, and sharpish too!

The little man approached me, eyes fired with drunken enthusiasm: 'Why mon, you're bloody great. I nivva knew opera was such fun. Would ye play for us on Frida in Ashington?'

'No thanks, I'm working every night this week.'

'We wouldn't need ye till 1.00 am like.' He saw the interest in my face. I would be finished at around 11.00 pm and was staying just four miles from Ashington. 'I'll gie ye thawty poon,' he said.

'No!'

'Fawty.'

'No!'

'I'll gie ye fifty for twenty minutes.'

'Done!' I pencilled *Cleansing Department Annual Ball* into my diary.

When I arrived around midnight the place was a swinging uproar; I'm sure I was the only sober person in the place. My little friend met me at the door: 'Come in an have a drink, it's ahl free.'

At 1.00 am, feeling a little rosy, I suggested perhaps I should get ready to perform. 'Why noah lad;—the Geordie 'noah' is not the famous boat builder, simply the negative—'have another drink, nae hurry.'

By 1.30 am I knew that if I did not get on stage I never would. I put it to him. 'Listen lad,' said he quietly, 'I've decided not to bother.' I could barely hear him above the singing and stamping of feet.

'What about my money?'

'Dinna worry lad,' he said, paying me across the table in £10 notes. Singing *You'll never walk alone*, the 'lads' carried out my equipment. Hanging around my neck in a great display of affection—and to remain upright— my little friend escorted me to the car: 'I couldna' put ye on,' he slurred, 'they were enjoying themselves—y'd a spoilt it.'

Denis Tuohy

JOURNALIST AND BROADCASTER

The place, Durban, South Africa. The time, 1973.

I was making a film for Thames Television's *This Week* programme on the anti-apartheid strikes by black municipal workers. The atmosphere in the city was tense, threatening to explode at any moment into widespread inter-racial violence. One night as I returned to my hotel, I heard a familiar song drifting out from the windows of a popular cabaret.

'And we're off to Dublin in the green, in the green...'

I went inside to find a Belfast folk-rock group wowing their South African audience. I sent a message inviting them to join me for a drink at the interval.

When we met, I asked the age-old question about which foot they were digging with.

'Three taigs and three prods,' said the leader, 'total integration.'

'Terrific,' I said.

'Fantastic,' he agreed. 'The *Rand Daily Mail* had a feature about us yesterday. You should have seen the headline. 'The Integrated Pop Group from Ulster.'

'Wonderful,' I said and then, picking my words carefully, 'but isn't it ironic that you should be complimented on integration in South Africa of all places?'

The leader looked at me in amazement.

'What are you talkin' about, Denis? In South Africa they don't give a *damn* what religion you are.'

Anna Manahan

ACTRESS

In 1977 I came to London to play Bessie Burgess in 'The Plough and the Stars' at the National Theatre. I was staying in a hotel in a noisy and slightly hysterical area of central London and not much enjoying it when, to my great good fortune, the basement flat in Cyril Cusack's house became vacant. Cyril invited me to supper to meet the outgoing tenant and view the flat.

After a delicious meal and no small quantity of equally delectable vino, Cyril drew the curtains that we might view the pretty garden bathed in moonlight. I looked out and—lo and behold—saw the Virgin Mary standing at the end of the garden. I gawped, astonished. Not her, she smiled and after the initial surprise her face softened into an expression of great serenity.

I gripped Cyril. Was I seeing things? 'No,' said Cyril calmly, 'you are not. She's been here for three weeks now. Solid mahogany. I rescued her when they demolished a Catholic school!'

TH - E

65

Cyril Cusack

SCENE
St Joseph's Roman Catholic Church, Mexican Quarter,
Los Angeles—Mrs McVarish and Actor, Mobilhome
(luxury coach)—Day.

The Actor, clad as Cardinal, stands by the door of his
Mobilhome. Mrs McVarish, a small, shabbily-dressed,
middle-aged lady is seen approaching. She is carrying a
large item wrapped in coarse brown paper. She thrusts
the package at the 'Cardinal' who uncovers it to reveal a
huge wooden crucifix.
MRS McVARISH
(with an ingratiating smile):
'Would you bless this for me, Father?'
THE ACTOR
(confused but pleased):
'Well certainly—I mean, I'd like to very much, but, you
see I'm not a Cardinal; I mean I'm not even a priest—I'm
an actor.'
MRS McVARISH
(delighted):
'Are ye Father!'

'Spike' Milligan
COMEDIAN, WRITER AND BROADCASTER

Irish diver at the bottom of the sea.

Voice from ship: Come up, come up right away, Mick!
Mick: What for?
Voice from ship: The ship is sinking.

Ulick O'Connor

NOVELIST AND SHORT STORY WRITER

I won the Irish Championships in the pole vault in Balmoral Park, Belfast, in 1947. I was then 18 years of age. If I had known what I was letting myself in for I would have chucked the pole in the Lagan.

This pole was 16′ long and did *not* make an ideal travelling companion. When you arrived in a strange city the first thing to do was to find a pillar to hide your pole behind. Then you stood a fair chance of hailing a taxi. As you moved off you would reach out the window, grab the pole and hold it against one of the door handles while you kept your other hand in your ear, so as not to hear the driver's language. Manchester taxi-drivers would not take your pole on any account. They would frequently make suggestions as to what to do with the pole but these never included accepting it as freight.

This was nothing to the problem of competing in Scotland. I remember boarding a steamer returning from a Highland Games in the Isle of Bute. A disgruntled pipe-band—losers in the afternoon's competitions—played plaintive laments on the deck. I was carrying my pole and an Ayrshire carpet I had won and couldn't see where I was going. As I boarded, my pole pierced a bagpipe: there was a sound like a scalded cat's scream, the piper near burst, words flowed like lava, the band gathered, things turned nasty. I pointed to some boxing symbols on my blazer. This only drove additional Scots to his aid. Fortunately, at this point the captain offered me his protection, escorting me to safety when we reached the shore.

I once took my pole to Germany. Getting off at Bonn I asked the porter to give me my pole from the luggage van. I only knew one German word, the one for pole. He stuck out his tongue. I shrieked and held my arms as wide as I could to show what I was looking for. He thought I meant something else and put his hands in his ears and wagged them. The pole steamed off in the direction of Italy. I am happy to record that I never got it back.

Eamonn Andrews

BROADCASTER

A long time ago I aspired to be a Cyril Cusack and joined dear old Ria Mooney's School of Acting. On one occasion she was rash enough to give me a part in the one-act curtain-raiser preceding the main event at the Gaiety.

Final dress rehearsals were in progress. I was playing the part of a young suitor. Two daughters were on stage, plus mother, plus me. Mother had a touch of the vapours. Suitor (me), taking command of the situation, called for a cushion. Only what came out was the Dublin version, which is something like 'keschunn'.

'Stop!' roared Ria from the back of the theatre. 'The word is *"Cooshion". "Coooshion".'*

Performance time came and my ears were still red with embarrassment. I stood in the wings, awaiting my cue repeating . . . *'cooshion', 'cooshion', 'cooshion'.*

On I sailed. In due course my lady had her vapours and I called exquisitely for a 'cooshion'. Fine. Only I should have called for a glass of water.

The cushion bit came three pages later but my fellow novices, Pavlov-trained, skipped the intervening and vital explanation of the plot to produce the cushion.

No-one from the doubtless baffled audience has ever mentioned it to me since.

J.G. Devlin

ACTOR

Fonsie O'Toole was his name. He was a giant of a man, 6′ 5″ and about 24 or 25 stones. He was a great pint drinker and loved to eat potatoes and butter by the mountain—everything about the man was on a grand Falstaffian scale.

One day in 1927 old O'Hanlon died and we were all invited to the wake. Three houses were filled that night, his own and that of each of his neighbours. As the man's last edict had been the insistence that he 'go out with a bang not a whimper', there was a great good humour in the air; and why not, O'Hanlon had had a good innings and the odds weren't too long that he'd gone to a better place.

Now on these occasions it was the custom for the fellas to sit with their girls on their knees, for there were rarely seats for all. Fonsie was sat on a Bentwood chair—loaned by one of the neighbours—with a very beautiful girl on his knee. Nestled in Fonsie's expanse she enjoyed, I'm sure, the most comfortable seat in the house. Dainties were devoured and porter flowed.

The occasion was at its height when, as often happens, a silence descended, numerous apparently vigorous conversations simultaneously died. At this moment nature took its capricious course: Fonsie broke wind. Now as fate would have it the Bentwood chair is an excellent conductor of sound. But Fonsie was on his guard, and leaned on his side to get it out nice and gently, but the more he tried to hold it the more it forced its way out. By the time he gave up trying to syphon it he had attracted the whole room's attention. In quick succession there followed a massive unruly detonation and a sigh of contentment from Fonsie. Seismographs quaked all over Europe. As the last feeble notes died away, before anyone had yet breath to speak, Fonsie whispered to his girl, 'You can blame it on me.'

Jim Molyneaux

MP AND LEADER OF OFFICIAL UNIONIST PARTY

Responding to a request to call on a constituent, I arrived to find a large dog lying across her garden path. I trod warily, however the animal proved friendly and accompanied me to the door where we were both admitted by the lady of the house.

The arrival of a tea trolley attracted the dog's enthusiastic attention. With much tail wagging the beast polished off what remained of the chicken sandwiches, then slaked a fierce thirst by attempting to drink directly from the cream jug, with disastrous consequences. I could not help thinking my host was carrying her love of animals a bit far!

I somehow sensed that the atmosphere had become a little strained, but the reason did not become clear until I had taken my leave. On reaching the gate I heard the lady of the house call: 'Mr Molyneaux, aren't you taking your dog with you?'

Ian Paisley

MP, EUROPEAN MP AND LEAD OF THE 'DUP'

Before going to prison in 1966 I was given a thorough medical examination. After the doctor had run the stethoscope over me he took a step back and said, 'You're fit.'

'Indeed I am not,' I said, 'I'm Paisley.'

Gerry Fitt
SOCIALIST MP

In 1969 I went on a speaking tour of the USA. Anticipating two to three weeks abroad, I packed half a dozen of everything in the way of underwear which the well-dressed gent requires and flew via London to Los Angeles.

The meetings went smoothly, but the tour schedule was a shambles. We went from Los Angeles to New Jersey, then flew back to San Francisco, to a hall 40 minutes drive from one in which we'd had the original meeting. This carry-on left me no time to see to my laundry so whenever something got dirty I stuffed it into a plastic bag which I pushed into the depths of my suitcase. When we finally checked into the St Francis Hotel in San Francisco I was wearing my last set of clean clothes.

In the morning I rang for breakfast. A 6'4" no-English, Japanese attendant (honest!) wheeled in the trolley and left me to it. As I sat to eat I marvelled at the way the trolley heated my knees. Lifting the tablecloth I discovered a bunsen-burner affair busy keeping my egg and bacon warm: I had my masterstroke. Taking the plastic bag from my suitcase, I washed all my underwear in the bathroom and spread it to dry on the rail above the bunsen—replacing the table cloth in order to retain the heat.

Feeling generally pleased with myself I treated myself to a shower. I emerged just in time to see the door close—the trolley and my washing were gone! I

flung on a towel and gave chase. I met Odd-Job in the corridor. What could I want with my decimated breakfast? Was I a secret toast-crust fiend? I pulled at the trolley—he tugged back: it ground my foot—I howled.

Doors opened up and down the hall. I felt my towel working loose so I gave up the unequal struggle and hopped back to my room. Our next stop was Chicago—'The Windy City'. I can tell you I felt the breeze.

Larry Gogan
DISC JOCKEY

The average life of a disc jockey in Chicago is three years. It's dog-eat-dog and if you don't get the listeners you're out, which is why I like the story of Dan Sorkin, a Chicago DJ. The Nielson research organisation gave him a rating which in effect said that there wasn't anybody listening to him at all, so Dan undertook a campaign to save Rose Bimber. The station was swamped by bags of mail from distressed listeners. Soon there were 'Save Rose Bimber' clubs from coast to coast, balloons, stickers and even a song 'The Ballad of Rose Bimber'. There was no such person.

Maureen Potter

ACTRESS

Touring the Variety Theatres of Britain in the 1950s in wintertime could be a very chastening experience. We did two shows nightly at 6.15 pm and 8.45 pm. The first house in those difficult days consisted of a few rows of old age pensioners who sat in overcoats daring you to entertain them. My solo act of the young Irish dancer festooned with bogus medals—which had been a great success in Dublin left them very cold indeed in St Helens.

On the Wednesday night I was halfway through the act when a tall gaunt lady appeared by my side from nowhere. Even the orchestra began to pay attention. 'What do you want, love?' I asked, petrified.

'I'm looking for my mother,' she replied, in a doleful, quavering voice. I glanced down at my gym slip and dancing pumps.

'Well, I'm not you mother, love,' I told her nervously. The audience loved it. Terrified, I took the poor lady by the hand and led her off the stage. She disappeared into the night.

'Great stuff!' enthused the stage manager. 'Thank heavens you've changed your act.'

Bunny Carr

BROADCASTER

I remember one ghastly experience in a Dublin cafe. I was alone having a quick bit of nosh. I was hiding behind my newspaper. Behind it I was doing a fair job of packing in calories, digesting the letters to the editor at the same time.

I became aware of a 'giggle' of six school girls whispering very loudly about yours truly. Eventually one of the 15 year olds left the table at the other end of the restaurant. The other diners watched as she approached. She offered me a menu card to sign. I gulped down the most recent intake of steak and kidney and smiled. Not, I should imagine, a pretty sight. She read my signature and turned away. While she was still some ten feet from her mates she said, 'I told you he wasn't Terry Wogan.'

I cringed lower behind my paper. Take my word for it there is no way you can enjoy steak and kidney pie when you are guilty of not being Terry Wogan.

Terry, an old friend, has always had literary leanings. To this day, on a wooden partition in Belvedere College (where Terry defied the best efforts of the Jesuits to educate him) is carved the stark message 'T. Wogan'. They say it's the only work he completed there without a spelling error.

Terry Wogan

DISC JOCKEY AND BROADCASTER

One of the winsome traits of the Irish is their ability to deflate, with the cutting phrase, any manifestation in their fellow-man of affectation or self-regard.

As a boy announcer on RTE (Irish Television) the growth of a healthy ego was stunted by remarks such as: 'Look, it's your man—very *fat,* isn't he?' There was very little chance of becoming too big for your wellingtons, I can tell you.

However, the tale I tell is of my child-bride, the present Mrs Wogan, or as she likes to be known, *Blessed Helen of Maidenhead.* Some years ago, in a moment of uncharacteristic weakness on the part of some Kerryman, I was chosen to compere 'The Rose of Tralee' contest. Lady Wogan and I repaired to the kingdom's fair capital, and while I was rehearsing my merry banter, the Ladies Committee of the Festival of Kerry looked after Helen. They took her to the Festival Club, which featured music, booze and terpsichore in fairly even proportions.

In the corner, there was the making of a four-hand reel. One of the male dancers detached himself from the rest of the flying boots, and approached Helen: 'Excuse me, miss,' he requested, panting but civil, 'would you care to dance?'

Now, every well-brought-up young lady in Ireland knows that when you're asked to dance by a man, whether he looks like Quasimodo, smells like the wrath of God, or is footless with drink, it is not 'done' to refuse.

TH - F

However, having spent some time in foreign parts, and already tainted by life in Godless Britain, the wife said, 'No, thank you.' The world, or at the very least, Kerry, stood still. One of the unwritten laws of genteel Irish society had been cruelly cast in the dust. The erstwhile dancer was bemused, but only for a moment. He was, after all, carrying the banner of Irish manhood. He gave my wife a muted nod then turned to his friend and said loudly, 'Sure I was only being polite, she's much too old for me anyway . . .'

Val Mulkerns
NOVELIST AND SHORT STORY WRITER

A near relation of mine is, like myself, a peripheral figure on the stage of Irish writing; but unlike me Maurice Kennedy has written a story which everyone knows. It has been copiously translated and anthologised and is memorably titled *Vladivostock*. The author hasn't bothered to write anything since 1953; he says smugly he doesn't need to write any more.

I, on the contrary, have written hundreds of thousands of words whose exact form nobody can precisely remember. One evening I met a well-known television man—he shall be nameless—who staggered me by remembering one of my stories. He intended, if I agreed, to dramatise it for his channel. He said that he appreciated there were ethical difficulties attendant on my providing a play for television. I have for twelve years filled a TV column in an evening newspaper. However he thought this ethical reservation existed mainly in my own mind and could, indeed must, be overcome. He was, he said, a determined man.

For some minutes it was impossible to get a word in edgeways. I opened my mouth several times but the sound came out of his. Finally I enquired, 'Which one?' He looked surprised then smiled, 'What a question! *Vladivostock,* of course.'

W. D. Flackes
POLITICAL CORRESPONDENT

'The Russian Embassy is on fire!' said the news editor. 'I want a report Billy, fast.' So shortly before 4.00 pm I took a taxi to Kensington Palace Gardens, or KPG as it is known in diplomatic circles. It hosts a score of diplomatic buildings and has an air of intrigue beloved of spy thriller writers. The Russian Embassy has always had a mysterious aura, it was all the more pronounced on this occasion, this was the height of the Stalin era. I snuggled into my seat and wondered what was in store.

As I approached the hoses were just getting to work. A quick glance was enough to establish that the blaze was not extensive. There was no-one in the foyer. As time was of the essence I rang immediately for the Press Attache—get his statement, get to a phone, get out. A small porter stepped from the shadows and ushered me into an ante-chamber. No other reporters. Good. The door closed—did I hear a key turn? I tried the handle. Locked! What was happening?

I was locked inside for what seemed like ages. When they let me out I saw from their archway clock that it was only 5.15 pm. Still time! The attache handed me a statement and apologised profusely and politely for my accidental incarceration. I hurried to the phone and began dictating the story. I was interrupted by the news editor and told in no uncertain terms that he was already familiar with the story. He had read it in the *Evening News*. 'B ...b ..but ...' I began. He replaced the receiver. I met the porter on the steps and told him the story.

'I can't understand how he got it,' I told him, 'it's only 5.15 pm.'

He laughed, 'It's half past eight. That clock hasn't worked in thirty years!'

Billy Simpson

COLUMNIST 'BELFAST TELEGRAPH'

Until 1963 any job interview I'd been involved in had been on a one-to-one basis. In that year the paper I worked for ceased publication. One of my applications involved an interview by panel: nature's way of letting you know what a hanging jury looks like. At the end of a lengthy interrogation I turned to leave and found myself faced with two doors side by side. Determined not to give an impression of indecisiveness I gambled, walked straight into a broom cupboard and closed the door behind me. I suspect it was not this alone that lost me the job; it may have been the fact that I stayed in there for several minutes toying with the idea of never coming out.

Rowel Friers

CARTOONIST

Some years back I was designing a set for *Luther* at the Lyric Theatre, Belfast. This involved a considerable amount of hard work and buckets of perspiration. Undoubtedly the most onerous task was the creation of a massive crucifix. The cross was around the ten foot mark and the figure of Christ six foot six. To make the figure I used laminated polystyrene and carved it in traditional form, as the period dictated. The image I aimed to create was that of solid bronze and, in all modesty, I am forced to admit that the result was breathtakingly life-like.

Working in the entry at the side of the theatre, I was putting a last touch of spray to the big toe when a binman stopped to see what was going on. As he halted, the evening sun slid behind a cloud and a sudden breeze sprung up. As the breeze rose so did the deceptively heavy figure. As I leapt forward to prevent the ascension, I saw the binman pale visibly, cross himself and depart extremely rapidly: leaving me with a relieved expression, a six foot six bronze in my arms and a prayer of thanks in my heart.

William Trevor

NOVELIST AND PLAYWRIGHT

Before I was fortunate enough to make a living by writing I experienced considerable difficulty in finding jobs, holding jobs down and indeed making sense of any job I was fortunate enough to be offered. After I left Trinity College I answered an advertisement in the *Irish Independent* which stated that someone was needed to teach a backward child to read. 'Suit a nun' it said. I got the job. But I couldn't live on thirty shillings a week and soon afterwards I found myself in Co. Armagh, in a prep school that almost immediately went bankrupt. Hard pressed again, I found a job writing advertisements in London. Here I touched what may well be the rock-bottom of human endeavour. Finding something to say, interesting or otherwise, about reverse-threaded screws was far from easy, and nothing improved when I attempted to engage my talents on behalf of Sanderson's renowned wallpapers and fabrics.

'We are sending you to New York,' an account executive announced, 'to take photographs and to write about the latest in American decor. You must visit the beige and pumpkin-coloured apartment of Mrs Garner Karsh and many similar. We must get across the feeling that Sanderson are constantly in touch with the best in decor all over the world.'

We went, a small bespectacled photographer and myself. We photographed Mrs Garner Karsh's beige and pumpkin-coloured apartment, and I did my best to write about it. We photographed Mrs Garner Karsh herself, and Mrs Patti Chast and Mrs Arthur K. Handlesman, all of whom were in the decor business. Then I discovered young Mr Thiebaud, who was said to be better than any of them.

Unfortunately, the night before we were to visit Mr Thiebaud the photographer discovered whiskey sours and ended up on the Bowery, in search of local colour. His money, spectacles, most of his clothes and his camera were stolen from him. As far as I was concerned, the money and the clothes didn't matter but the spectacles and the camera did rather. I arrived at the Thiebaud apartment with a hired camera and a photographer who was to all intents and purposes blind. Mr Thiebaud told me he called his apartment the 'Seasonal Apartment' and that he had designed all its wall papers himself, his theme being Passing Time. I led the photographer around by the elbow and did my best to focus his camera for him. 'We work very closely,' I explained. Mr Thiebaud and I then sat down to interview.

Between us there was what used to be called a *pouffe* and perhaps still is. It was covered with a light, rather attractive leather, and I asked permission before leaning my notebook on it in order to jot down Mr Thiebaud's valuable answers to my questions. Somewhere behind me his secretary was arranging vases of flowers, which the photographer kept bumping into and apologising to, in case they were people. To my horror I heard him informing the secretary that he was thirsty. Fortunately, at this point Mr Thiebaud left.

Amidst the din of crashing vases I noticed the condition of the *pouffe*. It was a humid morning and quite a number of my ballpoint notes had unfortunately transferred themselves to the leathery surface. I spat and rubbed but nothing happened.

I chatted to the secretary, who was disposing of broken glass in the kitchen. Behind my back I felt for a damp cloth and found one in the sink. But when I conveyed it to the *pouffe* the marks didn't go away so I returned to the kitchen and chatted again. I felt about for a detergent and managed to spill some onto my cloth. I returned to the *pouffe* and when I rubbed really hard the ballpoint marks began to come off. I also took off the attractive surface, which was not leather but some kind of plastic on a canvas backing. While I placed a painted wooden duck over the quite sizable hole, the photographer walked into another vase of flowers.

We left New York as quickly as possible after that. The photographs of Mr Thiebaud's 'Seasonal Apartment' were not good but no complaints about our visit drifted across the Atlantic from Mr Thiebaud. In gratitude I wrote glowingly of his genius as a designer of wallpapers, employing a dazzling selection of superlatives. Not until the advertisements had actually appeared in the Sunday supplements did I discover that Mr Thiebaud was a manufacturer of wallpapers. He was Sanderson's main rival in New York.

Christy O'Connor

GOLFER

During the Carroll's Tournament at Woodbrook some years ago, it rained and rained. After completing the third round in a sort of deluge that inspired Noah, Neil Coles and I squelched into the locker room to change our clothes.

I think the rain had beaten the conversation out of both of us, anyway, neither of us had much to say. I started unlacing my shoes in silence, puddles forming round my feet. Behind us, from the far side of the wall of lockers, we heard the following:

'God I suffer for this game.'

'Don't talk. That pair are the very limit.'

Nigh invisible beneath our protective plastic, we watched the two men leave the room. Having character assassinated their foolhardy paymasters, our caddies headed towards the bar: doubtless to inoculate themselves against the prospect of *a further thirty-six holes* with *us* tomorrow.

Jack Lynch

TD AND FORMER TAOISEACH

A few weeks after my appointment to the Ministry of Education, I was invited to officially open the *Blarney Tostal* (Spring Festival). I arrived at Blarney resplendent in my short black jacket, striped morning trousers and trilby hat. Having reviewed the guard of honour I made my opening address to a gathering of several hundred on Blarney's very picturesque village green. I was then invited to throw in the ball to start a junior hurling match between two young local teams. At that time eight players from each team lined up in the centre of the pitch, the ball was thrown between them and the match began.

Having had plenty of experience of this in my own playing days I made an effort to project the ball into the centre of the lines of players. Immediately I was fascinated by how deftly one of the young combatants took the ball on his stick, smartly avoided three tackles, and weaved around the back of the line towards me. I should immediately have run off, but this lad's prowess seemed to mesmerise me. Before I had time to gather my wits he was facing me and about to strike for goal. Should I dash sideways, duck, step back? I decided to step back, but caught in three minds I acted too late: my feet went from under me, and I fell—with a singular lack of grace.

My newly-pressed morning suit and black trilby hat absorbed quite a quantity of village green mud. Not a very auspicious start for a new Minister, I reflected, especially one who had enjoyed some reputation on the hurling field. I got to my knees, recovered my hat, my composure, and left the pitch—to the great delight of the locals, who seemed to think it was the best performance they'd seen from a government minister in years.

Mary O'Hara

SINGER

I was en route to New Zealand for a six week tour and the plane was droning along nicely. I reflected that if the New Zealand audiences were as warm and enthusiastic as the Australian ones had been all would be well. Comforted by this prospect I dozed off and didn't wake until the plane touched down.

As one of the first to descend to the tarmac, I couldn't but notice a sizeable group of people—some clutching bouquets of flowers—standing in a sort of hushed expectancy and gazing in my direction. 'Good gracious,' I thought, 'how touching.'

Beaming broadly I advanced towards the throng, radiating suitable appreciation and permitting myself modest gestures of acknowledgement. As the space between us diminished I noticed no smiles to meet my own. Undaunted I pressed on, after all, they might all be short-sighted. Suddenly they burst into life. I responded with my most engaging smile. I was quite close now, however not a single beatific gaze was directed my way. I stole a quick glance over my shoulder; the Russian Ballet Company were descending from the plane.

Harry West
FARMER AND POLITICIAN

My career as a Stormont MP became intensely interesting in 1958 when Lord Brookeborough appointed me Parliamentary Secretary to the Ministry of Agriculture. One of my first calls was to be present when the Minister received six ladies from the Housewife's League to discuss the vexed question of the quality of bacon. When the great moment arrived he took up a position just inside the door and shook hands with each lady as she entered. When the promised number of six had been exceeded by about ten—and the officials were hurriedly chasing round looking for extra chairs—the Minister raised both hands, called the officials to a halt and announced that they were not to bother any further because the ladies would not be staying. Amidst much heated argument he ordered the party out of his office.

Very unfortunately the Minister was shortly after taken to hospital and I—a junior with little experience—found myself temporary political head of the largest Ministry in the Stormont administration.

The President of the Housewife's League paid me an early visit. In an attempt to make amends for the former debacle, I promised to address a meeting of her 'girls'. When the day came, I proceeded with some trepidation to the meeting. From the platform I observed 52 stern looking middle-aged ladies waiting to be enlightened on a subject which I knew precious little about.

Unfortunately, I got the idea that if I could preface my remarks with a story, it might make my task somewhat

lighter. In my opening remarks I suggested that in many areas community relations were much better than the media would have us believe and mentioned a housing estate near my home in which both 'sides' lived very happily. In fact, I went on, I knew of one semi which had a Catholic couple—who had a boy of 3 or 4 years of age—on one side, and a Protestant couple—with a girl of about the same age—on the other.

A very sincere friendship developed between these couples and they regularly travelled together to the seaside on a good Sunday afternoon. The families spread their rugs on the sand while the children ran off to paddle in the sea. On one occasion a big wave drenched both children. Their parents did the sensible thing—they stripped off the children's clothes and let them loose. As the children were running down the sand to the water, the little Protestant girl eyed the Catholic boy. Suddenly she ran back to her mother and in an agitated whisper confided: 'Mummy I think daddy's really a Catholic.'

The story was greeted with stony silence. My sole comfort was a weak smile from the lady on the extreme left of the front row and when she saw nobody else seemed amused, she hastily re-assumed her grim set, leaving me with the rather doubtful pleasure of laughing at my own joke.

Frank Carson–Again!

My father and I were waiting in a taxi on the Falls Road, staring vacantly at a helicopter floating five or six miles away.

'It's been like that for ten minutes or more,' observed father.

'Yeah,' said I absent-mindedly, 'maybe it's broken down.'

TH – G

Sinead Cusack

ACTRESS

At twenty I came to London to seek my fortune. Fortunes were thin on the ground in those days and a couple of years of unemployment followed. But at twenty-two my fortunes changed, I was offered a starring role opposite Peter Sellers in a film called *Hoffman*. Film stardom, I was assured, was mine for the taking. Well, the film may perhaps have been successful in Stoke Poges but the Great British Public didn't take it to their hearts and the critics were even less kindly disposed.

I, however, remember the experience with affection. I recall a few days spent filming in the meat department of Harrods with particular joy; Peter and I acted out many tender moments there amongst its gracefully hung carcasses.

Many months of gainful unemployment later, dreams of stardom rapidly diminishing, I decided to cheer myself up by giving my first dinner party. I remembered my mother serving fillet of beef on high days and holidays at home: this was the dish with which to delight my guests! To add further spice to the occasion I decided that I would buy the meat at Harrods.

I was greeted with open arms by the many butchers there. News of the film's failure had not yet filtered through. I was seen as an ascending star and my request was instantly attended to.

'The whole fillet, Madam?' the 'maitre' gently enquired.

'Oh yes, and have it delivered!' I declared, aglow with pride at being remembered for the star I had never become. So aglow, it wasn't until I got home that I discovered I had bought the whole hind!

Stewart Parker

PLAYWRIGHT

I was in a tiny Dublin restaurant with some friends a few days after the opening of a play of mine at the theatre festival. The daily reviews had been excellent, and it only remained to see what the Sunday papers said. We were all raucously merry, and the conversation turned to the critic of a London Sunday. It was agreed that he would probably pan the play because he was a sour, mean-spirited creep. I added the information that he had once been turned down for a television job in favour of the play's director. Others commented on the comicality of his appearance. I became aware of a curious atmosphere in the place. I turned round; the man was finishing his dinner at the table directly behind me.

You're right. He panned the play.

Martin Smyth
GRAND MASTER OF THE
ORANGE LODGE OF IRELAND

At school I served as a sergeant in the Army Cadet Force. During camp one year I told the lads in my squad of an incident some years previously when a University OTC unit had carried their major from his hut, and left him fast asleep amidst the cattle in a neighbouring field.

Several nights later, I had a sensation of being moved. However when I awoke with reveille, I was in the hut with my pals.

The story soon came out.

They were moving me during the night, when, though fast asleep I had apparently murmured, 'Don't boys, you'll only have to carry me back.' They let my bed down smartly and jumped back to their own. Seeing I was dead to the world they crawled out again and this time left me outside.

Apparently, as the more wily of you may have anticipated, the regular guard saw me, put two and two together and made them carry me back. I remained sweetly oblivious.

One evening during that same camp a group of us were relaxing in Newcastle having fun. Some began making dares and naturally some were taken up. One fellow dared any of us to walk up to a group of girls and kiss one. Strong stuff! (Things weren't quite as informal as today.) No one was ready to take it up until amongst a group of girls, I recognised an old friend whom, I believed, might respond positively to my overtures.

Boldly, to the amazement of my associates, I approached—from the rear, a good military tactic if at all possible. I grabbed the girl, swung her round and kissed her. Horrors! She was a total stranger!

Cardinal Tomas O'Fiaich

CARDINAL, ROMAN CATHOLIC ARCHBISHOP OF
ARMAGH AND PRIMATE OF ALL-IRELAND

After a late meeting in Dublin on a rainy January night, I went to Marlborough Street to collect my Morris Minor, to find the back wheel was flat. I began to change the wheel in the pelting rain. It was a dirty job, slow and exhausting. One after another, cars drove out of the car-park and passed gaily by. I was thinking bitterly of the parable of the Good Samaritan when I noticed a small ragged figure emerge from the pub across the street. He caught sight of me. He wasn't too steady on his feet, but he made it across.

'Are you in trouble, Father?' says he, and stood chatting till the job was done. I gave him a little reward for his pains, trying to balance it neatly between what wouldn't appear mean and what wouldn't be sufficient to set him drunk. I set the car in motion and he returned to the shelter of the pub.

Next day Cardinal D'Alton died and was lamented by the whole people. Thousands lined O'Connell Street as the funeral procession moved slowly towards the Parnell Monument. Now another Armagh priest had offered me a lift in his Volkswagen, and not wishing to travel north without a spare-wheel I had gladly accepted. As we approached the GPO the car began to chug.

'Go over to the spare gallon, Gerry,' I shouted, sensing that we were running low.

Gerry gave the lever a kick. 'Good God,' he exclaimed, 'I'm on it already!' The car came to a halt

before the GPO.

'We're ruined,' I thought, looking at the line of prelates and Ministers of State who had been brought to a halt behind us. There seemed to be nothing for it except to get out and heave the car out of the way of the Mercedes and Daimlers that were already hooting for the road. Suddenly I saw a little figure emerge from the crowd, on his face, the faintest suspicion of a smile. It was unmistakably my friend of the previous night.

'Don't get out or they'll recognize you,' he called, as he started pushing us out of the traffic.

The line of cars passed but we saw very little of the funeral as we were both bending down to search for non-existent objects under the seats.

A half-hour was enough to get a tin of petrol, reward our good Samaritan and catch up with the funeral before it reached Armagh. As we prayed for the Cardinal's soul in the Cathedral that night, I felt he was also being prayed for in a pub in Marlborough Street.

Maeve Binchy
JOURNALIST AND AUTHOR

To understand fully the nightmare you must know that I am by any standards a large woman, and that the Chinese people are by most standards very small.

Right. I was in Taiwan on a business trip, and far from it being glitter and the magic of the Orient, it was horrific. So there I was, marooned in my dull hamburger-only hotel, getting lonely and bored. It was not acceptable for lone women to go prowling the narrow streets of Taipei: I forced myself to be courageous. Why should I eat bad hamburgers instead of real Chinese food?

The cafe was very full. I sat down and a bewildered looking waiter handed me a menu. Now in Taiwan you can't start talking about a portion of number 37, you have to say what you want or point to it on the menu.

I was so afraid that I might be given bat, or seaweed, or rice pudding that I did what I thought was very resourceful, I got up and pointed to the meal of a man who was eating sweet and sour prawns. The waiter nodded gravely. Flushed with success, I went over to another table and pointed to a glass of beer. He nodded again.

Back at my table I took out my book and felt very proud of myself. Not everyone could go to the heart of a different culture and order a meal so successfully, I thought. This is what international understanding is all about. Resourcefulness. I gave a little sigh of pleasure.

To my horror I saw the waiter wrestling the plate of

sweet and sour prawns away from the man who had been about to eat them. Some words were exchanged in Chinese and then the dish was laid in front of me. Helpless, I watched the other man hand over his beer without even putting up a fight. All around the restaurant people glared at me through narrow, baleful eyes.

The waiter looked at me nervously. I stood up to try and explain, but I felt I looked more menacing standing up, my shadow seemed to fall over the whole restaurant. So I sat down. The waiter loosened his collar and looked at me as if begging me to eat. At least that's what I thought. Using finger and chopstick I shovelled down some sweet and sour prawns. I smiled to show that I thought they were excellent. The waiter relaxed, people went back to their meals.

The men whose drink and food I was eating didn't seem to get any replacements. I was afraid to look at their faces.

There was no question of money. When I took out some Taiwanese dollars, the waiter looked at me fearfully. I sort of backed out of the restaurant smiling and waving like a lunatic entertainer, and ran for my life back to 'Hamburger Hotel'.

Derek Bell

MUSICIAN

Owing to the strange political beliefs of our Ministry of
Education in the 30s and 40s I learnt virtually no Irish.
We were giving a concert at the Colaiste Mhuire where
one is encouraged to speak Irish all the time, and sure
enough, a well meaning fellow came up and addressed
me in a long tirade of beautifully fluent Dublin Irish, not
a word of which I understood. I had just returned from
playing some piano concertos in Hungary, so not to be
outdone, I replied to our friend in an even longer tirade of
Hungarian: including the string of swear words which
were my first acquaintance with the language. Then in
my most superior tone I'm reputed to have said: 'Oh, I
beg your pardon, you good Dublin folk may not
understand our Northern dialect.'

'On the contrary,' he replied *in Hungarian*—I think he
understood only too well.

Seamus De Burca

THEATRICAL COSTUMIER

My uncle often had the task of delousing some of the hovels of cottages which abounded in the laneways of Dublin when I was a boy. He was very proficient and his expertise was widely admired. There was an infested room in the Imperial Hotel in O'Connell Street and they asked him to eradicate the scourge—unfortunately it was not until the 1916 fire that the problem was solved!

The good man once took me to a flea circus near the Corinthian Cinema; this greatly enhanced my respect for the flea. I saw them harnessed to chariots, riding bicycles and pulling steam rollers ten times their weight.

They lived on humans. Each flea daily sucked three times its own weight of blood from its master's wrist—the fleas I knew did not confine themselves to my wrist!

I remember in Killelan I was troubled with fleas in the bed. I discussed the subject with Jack O'Neill and was solemnly advised to use this method of getting rid of the pest: wrap a hot brick in red flannel and place it in the bed about an hour before you retire. When you are about to get in remove the brick and flannel, run downstairs and deposit the flannel in the fire. *If this doesn't work you are at liberty to throw the brick at Jack O'Neill's head!*

I must say the vaunted formula did my fleas no harm, so if you have more fleas than you can manage with comfort don't take Jack O'Neill's cure; neither do I recommend placing a saucer of beer in the bed, expecting the flea to drown itself. If you have any beer *Drink it yourself man and ignore the blasted fleas!*

Paddy Devlin

TRADE UNIONIST AND POLITICIAN

In 1974 Bernard Crick invited a colleague and I to speak in Birkbeck College, London, one lunchtime on the subject of Northern Ireland. Almost 200 people had assembled on the fourth floor and not all were students from the college's political faculty. This caused some concern.

Taking us to one side, Professor Crick told us that he didn't like the look of certain members of the audience: they had made trouble for him before.

'We'll make some arrangements for your protection,' he continued, 'we'll put a row of desks in front of the podium. When they rush you, the desks will delay them long enough for you to escape down the fire escape and lose yourself in the shoppers.'

I listened in astonishment. Something welled inside me. I blurted out that I wasn't going to run away. 'What'll you do if they rush you?'

'Biff the first man over those desks.'

'Are you serious?'

'Never more serious in all my life.'

A pause. 'I suppose you are entitled to defend yourself,' he reflected: then censoriously, 'It won't do my college's reputation any good.' He stared at me gravely, then whispered, 'but if you do, try to catch that little wretch with long, black hair. The wee ——deserves everything he gets!'

Fred Daly

GOLFER

Bobby Locke was notoriously slow on the greens. Worse, he had recently beaten me four times in a row. One day newly arrived Australian Norman von Nida asked me how come Bobby pipped me so often. In an effort to convey the towering frustration of a round with Bobby I replied:

'Norman I haven't much hair, a few more rounds with Bobby and I'll be bald.'

Curious as to how Norman found him I added:

'I hear you played him on Saturday.'

Norman said nothing. He took off his famous beret. He was bald.

Caroline Walsh

JOURNALIST

It was November 1975 and I was twenty-two. I wore my new green sweater and cord skirt. It was that golden moment of my youth, my first day at *The Irish Times*.

On arriving at 8.45 am sharp I found the newsroom completely deserted. I surveyed an unappealing panorama of leftover plates of chips and sodden cigarette butts in coffee. Where were all the hard-headed hacks? They rolled in around 10.00 am. By this time my confidence had given way to panic; fortunately, I was largely ignored until around noon. Then I was instructed to observe a senior reporter. Look and learn. I did.

The day passed slowly until just after 6.00 pm. A figure approached from the newsdesk. Would I like to go to a reception on the other side of town? Would I! Willingly! Oh, how nice! I thought. When I got there I found myself whisked from one dignitary to another while drink after drink was forced into my hand. A born socialiser, I had a happy time, so happy that rather than go straight home I thought I'd call into the office and thank them for the party. I began to tell them about the 'do' but I might have had amnesia for all I could remember.

The editor's polite request for copy interrupted my meander. Only then, bless my innocence, did it dawn on me that I had been out on my first job.

Conor Cruise O'Brien

EDITOR-IN-CHIEF OF 'THE OBSERVER'

I was Vice-Chancellor (academic head) of the University of Ghana from 1962–65. During that period I ran into considerable difficulties with the then President of Ghana, Kwame Nkrumah, who did not see eye to eye with me on matters affecting academic freedom and university autonomy. Matters reached such a point that the President was heard to remark: 'That fellow wants me to fire him, and that's why I am not going to do it.'

As my contract was expiring and neither party wanted to renew it, I arranged to pay a courtesy farewell call on the President. He agreed and had decidedly the better of the consequent exchange. The President's office in Christiansborg Castle was about the size of a tennis court. The President's desk was at the end most remote from the door. If you were in favour, as I had been, the President would come half-way down this expanse to meet you. If you were not you walked up to the desk. I walked up to the desk. The President was writing. After a few minutes he looked up from his papers. 'Ah . . . ,' he said, 'Dr O'Brien . . . I want to thank you, Dr O'Brien . . . for whatever it was you did for the University.'

After this encouraging start, we went on to discuss the vacant post of Vice-Chancellor. I urged that in the interests of the University this post should be speedily filled by somebody who had the confidence of the academic body. The President was of a different opinion. 'The filling of the post of Vice-Chancellor is an important matter to which I propose to devote considerable thought—*this* time, Dr O'Brien.'

History had the last word. The President was still devoting considerable thought to the filling of this important post when his own became vacant by military coup, seven months after the above conversation.

John Morrow

NOVELIST AND SHORT STORY WRITER

He asked for an 'egg-on-the-face' experience. I have decided to take the phrase at its literal meaning and relate the saga of my first drink. This occurred while I was still an apprentice lapper in the Belfast warehouse of an old-established linen manufacturer. It was what is called a 'family' firm, meaning that the warehouse was a mere satrap of a small empire stretching back to a 'Big House' deep in the boondocks of Armagh, close to a village which bore the 'family' name (because owned by the family) and within sight of the 'family' mill and bleachworks. The emperor himself, gout bound, ruled from the 'Big-House', the constituent elements of his realm being the responsibility of his three sons: Master Robert at the mill, Master James at the bleach works, and at the Belfast warehouse, young Master William, looney of the litter.

We of the lower depths seldom saw Master William. It was said of him that had he been born into a peasant community they'd have bricked him up in the roof-space. Emerging, luckily, where he did, he was an 'old boy' of five English Public Schools by dint of surviving no more than a term at any. Along the way he acquired their two main benefices: arrogance and accent.

Only on special occasions was Master William allowed on public view. One of these was the source of my downfall, the occasion being the retirement of an old journeyman after 35 years service to the family. Ned had been born and reared in the 'family' village, but had moved to the Belfast warehouse in his twenties and had remained there since, in bachelor digs, a lonely man in an always strange place whose fierce loyalty to the firm was a perennial wonder to we city sceptics. Of course, there was no such thing as a pension for Ned; but there was, that day, Master William saying how pleased he was and dropping a silver-plated pocket watch into his grateful hand. As always, Master William's keeper was close by, a shrewd 'family' retainer of good NCO stock, nominally warehouse manager, whose relationship with his charge I was to recognise later in P. G. Wodehouse's Jeeves/Bertie Wooster stories. Even he couldn't prevent Master William putting his foot in it . . 'You look simply *marvellous,* Ned,' he bayed at the withered wreck, 'I bet you last longer than that demmed watch, eh what!'

After he had been led away we all went to Robinson's in Great Victoria Street and got roaring drunk. I arrived home that evening and collapsed, face down, in the middle of a plate of Ulster Fry. I was carried to bed.

I wakened next morning with egg still caked on my face and promised my distraught mother that she'd never again see me in that state. She never did. I bought a rucksack and a pair of big boots and henceforth got drunk in the seclusion of the Mournes.

Ned lasted a year after retirement, nine months longer than the watch. Ten years later the 'family' empire was gobbled up by Mr Cyril Lord. With his share of the loot, Master William bought a chain of villas on the Costa del Chips. That's one 'economic target' I'd not begrudge the Basques.

116

Havelock Nelson

MUSICIAN

During my career as a pianist with the BBC it sometimes fell to my lot to play at auditions for would-be radio and television stars. One day during a session a highly nervous gentleman entered. He approached me with an apologetic air and said, 'Dr Nelson, I haven't got a copy of my song but I'm only going to sing "The Mountains of Mourne", would you impoverish an accompaniment for me?'

'What key do you sing in?'

'A low key,' he replied.

Guffawing quietly, I explained that that could cover a fairly wide range—did he know the note he started on? 'Oh yes!' he said. Taking a piece of string from his pocket, he put one end on the lowest bass note of the keyboard; the idea was the other end would fall on the note he was supposed to start on.

And sure enough it did!

John Broderick

NOVELIST AND CRITIC

Some years ago I shared a London publisher, John Calder, with Samuel Beckett. Passing through London on my way to Paris, I called on the publisher in his office in Brewer Street. When I told him where I was going, he remarked that he was going there on the following day. 'See you at the Dome', he remarked as I left.

Later that night it occurred to me that that was rather a vague appointment; as I wanted to discuss some business with him—he was more dilatory in his payment than most publishers, and that's saying a lot— I decided to ring his secretary and find out where he was staying in Paris.

'Oh, I think he stays with Beckett,' she airily explained.

'Where is that?' I enquired.

'Haven't a clue, dear,' she replied, in the manner of publishers' secretaries everywhere, and particularly in London.

In Paris I got in touch with Fergus Pyle, then Paris Editor of *The Irish Times*. The only one with access to Beckett in Paris, according to him, was Con Leventhal, and he gave me his telephone number. Leventhal was kind and helpful, as he always was, and after explaining that Beckett answered the telephone only between twelve and one every day, he gave me the author's address. Paris telephones are worse than Dublin ones, so I jotted down what I shall call number *XY Boulevard St-*

Jacques.

That evening I set off in a taxi with Eric Jourdan. Number *XY Boulevard St-Jacques* turned out to be a vacant lot. I got out and looked around. After all one can never be sure about writers; but there was no sign of any human habitation, not even an ash-can, in that dusty place.

'Well, there is a *Rue de Boulevard St-Jacques*', Jourdan explained. Number *XV Rue de Boulevard St-Jacques* turned out to be a Russian Orthodox church, bolted and padlocked. 'No, not there, I really don't believe he lives there,' Jourdan remarked when ! returned to the taxi, 'but there's a *Rue St-Jacques*. Perhaps it's there.'

XY Rue St-Jacques turned out to be a lunatic asylum. 'Ah, exclaimed Jourdan, jumping from the taxi, 'this I will investigate myself! This is getting interesting.'

Five minutes later he came back chuckling. 'The concierge was very helpful. He said it was remarkable the number of people who called looking for M. Beckett. You got his number wrong. The concierge has it. It is *WY Boulevard St-Jacques*. Enfin, off we go!'

Number *WY Boulevard St-Jacques* was a large, impersonal block of modern flats overlooking the Sante prison. In the hall were the usual bells with the names of the occupants. There were two marked S. Beckett. Which one to ring?

'I would give it up if I were you,' said Jourdan. We're becoming characters in a Beckett play.'

Of course Calder did not stay with Beckett, and I didn't get paid for a year.

James Graham

TRADE UNIONIST

After a cataract operation, I had just begun wearing a contact lens when I had occasion to travel to Co. Donegal to meet represenatives of an international company on business.

As I was leaving I discovered I had lost the lens, so I went back to the conference room in the hope of finding it. When I got there the Works Manager, Works Engineer and Personnel Manager were still there. When I told them of my problem, the four of us got on our hands and knees and began to explore the floor.

I was first on my feet, and just as I stood up, the General Manager passed the open door to see his managers on their knees before me. 'I know you are an experienced negotiator Mr Graham,' he said, 'but this is ridiculous!'

Sad to relate, the lens was never found.

Mary Kenny

JOURNALIST AND AUTHOR

Recently I was having lunch with an old colleague in *El Vino*. This restaurant-cum-wine bar in London's Fleet Street is noted for the stuffiness of its rules. *El Vino* does not admit gentlemen unless they are wearing neckties—it has ejected Lord Snowdon and David Frost—and does not serve unaccompanied ladies. This made it a famous battleground in the late 1960s, when the establishment was 'stormed' by a group of Fleet Street feminists. Alas, this was one male bastion which refused to fall; on the contrary, *El Vino* thrived on its stuffy reputation.

Anyway, during this luncheon I was expostulating to my colleague on the relationship between police and young people: 'Youngsters know nothing about using the right language,' I declared. 'If only they would be courteous, youngsters would find the police can be very nice.'

As an example I related an encounter I had witnessed between a young woman and a traffic policeman; whenever he prevented her from driving down a closed off street she began abusing him: 'Oh for F--- sake, P--- off,' she said.

'Well, I ask you . . .' I shrugged to my companion and was reaching delicately for my drink when I heard a voice from above and behind: 'Miss Kenny,' it rasped, 'we do not tolerate bad language from *ladies* in this restaurant. I'm afraid I must ask you to leave.'

John B. Keane

PLAYWRIGHT, ESSAYIST AND SHORT STORY WRITER

In the summer of 1963 my wife sent me to a neighbouring fowl store to purchase two ducks. We were expecting an important American impresario who had already paid me five hundred dollars for an option on my play, *Many Young Men of Twenty*. We had decided to cook him roast duck.

The meal was a resounding success, not because of the ducks, but because our guest had an immense appetite for stout, and an inexhaustible repertoire of really excellent anecdotes. As the meal wore on my wife and I exchanged nervous glances: should we or should we not make reference to his proposed production of the play?

We decided to play it by ear. If our visitor wanted to bring up the subject, that was his business. In the interim, we would do all in our power to make his stay with us an enjoyable one. We remarked upon his phenomenal capacity for stout and he gave us as hearty a laugh as one could wish to hear.

After the meal we retired to the bar, where, instead of a liqueur, he confounded us by declaring himself in favour of another pint of stout. When some friends entered I introduced him with a certain degree of pride: 'This is Mister Lieber. He's a Broadway producer.'

This statement was responsible for the loudest and most prolonged bout of laughter of the evening:

'I'm not Mister Lieber,' he said between guffaws, 'I'm

123

Frank Murphy, and I'm not a Broadway producer, I'm an insurance salesman.' We beheld him with shock and disbelief.

'Why didn't you tell us?' I asked.

'You never asked,' he said.

'I can't believe it,' I said.

'You'd better believe it.' The comment came from a pasty-faced fat man, who stood at the counter, toying with a whiskey: 'I'm Lieber.'

James Hawthorne

CONTROLLER OF NI BBC

I have one of those faces which can belong to any racial group, but usually to a group which is either in a minority or else is positively despised.

Thus when I am among Arabs, it is assumed I am Jewish. In Tel Aviv I was a suspected Palestinian. British Customs once took me for a Spaniard and in Turkey they accused me of being Japanese. I avoid Greek Orthodox areas if I can and I've had one or two sticky moments in Italy and India.

It all started years ago in Bedford Street, Belfast, one sunny afternoon on my way to Broadcasting House. I was, as they say, minding my own business, when I became aware of the approach of a vaguely friendly man who seemed to have met me somewhere before. He was, incidentally, the archetypal Ulster working-man of that period, complete with mandatory blue collar, Christian Endeavour raincoat and dunsher cap..

At this point I introduce a complication because I happen to have an identical twin brother; and that's why I respond, in a wholly respectful manner, to complete strangers. Even the most casual nod in my direction can produce a smile of bogus recognition, the assumption being that I am about to meet one of my brother's close friends who may be unaware of my existence. Most of my diplomatic skills were learned under such trying circumstances. But I digress.

In Bedford Street that day the twin brother factor did not play a significant part. However there might have been something in my accommodating manner which encouraged the stranger to grip my arm and exclaim: 'Ach for dear sake, aren't you Abraham Fundaminsky?'

'No,' I said. It was to be the first of four questions. He released my arm but his eyes probed a little deeper. His second was: 'Yer one of the Fundamisky brothers?'

'No,' I said. My denial puzzled him a little. One more try. 'Yer a Jew aren't ye?'

'No.'

Cheerfully he added: 'Do ye think this weather will keep up?' I forget my reply, but I never saw him again.

Shortly after that I was invited to a party in Kensington Road (Belfast I again add), where archetypal working men are thin on the ground. I knew it was to be a ritzy evening so I decided I would give my well-heeled hosts a touch of the Austin Reeds. Clearly it was an opportunity for my lightweight tropical reversible-washable real-Irish synthetic linen-look jacket. Normally it would have taken a brave man to wear such a garment east of the Lagan, but Kensington Road was special, and as I picked my way through the Sunbeam Alpines parked in the garden, I had a feeling I'd hit it right.

The party was in full swing. A firm of high class caterers had been engaged and a brace of swarthy waiters were moving through the seething, bejewelled mass with speed and precision.

I looked round for the host and at that moment fingers lightly gripped my elbow. I turned. The eyes did not smile but the mouth said: 'One whisky and soda, two gin and tonics and a vodka and lemon.' As I edged away the voice called: 'Plenty of ice!'

Eamon Kelly

STORY TELLER AND ENTERTAINER

Though it might not seem so, television and radio planners go to quite extreme lengths to delight and entertain their respective publics on Christmas Day. Many years ago, through some oversight, I was included in Radio Eireann's bumper Christmas billing. As the programme was pre-recorded before a live (ha!) audience I was permitted my liberty on the day and went for a long morning walk.

On the road between Coolock and Howth I came across an itinerant tent, alone and forlorn in a wet field. As I passed it, like chickens from under a hen's wing, two children poked their heads from its flap. They were hungry: 'Mister, will the shops be open soon?'

'Not today,' I told them, 'nor tomorrow.' They nearly cried.

I made up my sentimental mind there and then. Tonight I would bring something to the tent for the children and a few bottles of stout for the parents. Back home I cut slices of everything that was going and packed them in a cardboard box. Our eldest—he was about four at the time—volunteered to help. We set out and would not have found the tent in the darkness if they hadn't had their radio on.

'Dad,' said our eldest, 'that's you!' The Christmas special was going out to the nation! The boy—an ardent fan of mine—was extremely pleased and proud.

We entered. The head of the family—out of courtesy—turned off the radio. They were delighted with the hamper: the children dressed up in the bright paper hats and tucked into the Christmas fare. Moving to go, and I must confess, in the hope that the man would turn on the radio—that I might have an opportunity to modestly reveal my identity—I remarked: 'You needn't have turned off the radio.'

'Ah,' he shrugged, 'it's all right, there was nothing on.'

Betty Lowry

WOMAN'S EDITOR 'BELFAST TELEGRAPH'

I was feeling rather pleased with myself. My morning mail had included two, yes two, letters complimenting me on a recent feature on my page in the *Belfast Telegraph*. A reader who telephoned the office to speak to me was surprised to be put through immediately to the Women's Editor: 'Is that really Betty Lowry? I thought I'd have to speak to a secretary first.' To cap it all I was taken to lunch by a public relations man; I was beginning to feel like a bit of a celebrity.

On the way back to the office we called in at a small shop, the kind you still find not far from the city centre. The owner had just mopped her tiled floor and covered it with newspapers while it dried. The man knew her and introduced us. 'This is Miss Betty Lowry ... I'm sure you know the name.' She looked blank for a second then said, 'I've seen that name. Now where ...?'

As she spoke she bent down and began scanning the newspapers on the floor. Then, pointing triumphantly to a 'By Betty Lowry' almost obliterated by a large muddy footprint, she said, 'There! I knew I'd seen it. Isn't that funny? I never heard of you till this morning and now you come into the shop ...'

TH - I

129

James Galway

FLAUTIST AND AUTHOR

My grandfather, another James Galway, came to live
with us during the last years of his life. In his day he had
been well known as a flute player, as had his father
before him.

I remember, as a small child, lying in bed listening to
my grandfather playing softly on his flute downstairs.
He had a few tunes that he was particularly fond of, and
he would often sit playing them well into the night.

When he died we had a wake. The family and neighbours gathered, and the table was set with a plentiful
supply of food and drink, not all of it soft. Apparently,
it upset me to see my poor grandfather lying all
neglected in his box (the coffin lid was still off),
particularly when everybody else in the room was busy
drinking and stuffing their faces. So, dutiful grandson,
I got a cheese sandwich and began feeding it to my
grandfather. By the time my mother discovered what
was afoot the poor man had half a cheese sandwich
stuck between his teeth. My mother's start drew my
father's attention. The man had a sense of humour:
'Count yourself lucky,' he roared, 'the chile mighta fed
him the whiskey!'

Graham Marshall

MUSICIAN

In March our old Ford Transit packed up just north of Birmingham and never moved of its own accord again. Our first job on our return was to find a new van, and pronto, for we had a date in Cork in two weeks.

Ten day later: no van. I was beginning to think we might have to hire something when I saw a van for sale in the 'Belfast Telegraph', priced just inside our range. A Godsend! We inspected it and though we didn't much like the look of the vendor, the van itself seemed sound. We thought about it, test drove it, discussed it and two days later parted with our cash.

The big day came. We all climbed in: she wouldn't budge. If it wasn't for our milk man and his high powered diesel (which we were sorely tempted to hijack) we might not have got started at all.

All went well until Drogheda. Here the brakes revealed themselves in their true colours and it was all we could do to avoid playing dodgems with a random selection of our fellow road users. This was nothing to what was in store! There followed a catalogue of disasters that has surely no rival in the history of the automobile—numerous stallings, flat tyres, a 30 mile tow and two visits from the AA man, who, after taking 45 minutes to get out to us, told us in a voice of great authority that the engine definitely would not start. Somehow—don't ask me—it started. The minutes ticked away, we had to be in Cork by 10.00 pm. In emergencies I'm possessed by this urge to sing nursery rhymes. At this point I started trilling and continued pretty well non-stop until Cork. When we arrived, at about 10.30 pm, we were surprised to hear a band playing. The promoter came out to greet us:

'What are you doing here lads, we booked you for next week.'

Vincent Browne

EDITOR OF 'MAGILL'

Matt and Gerry O'Brien were cousins of my grandfather. Matt (a draper), lived in Drumcollogher, and
Gerry lived on the family farm on the hill at the back of
my home village, Broadford. Both were bachelors and
both somewhat eccentric.

Matt had a sign in his shop window: 'Best jams,
underwear and habits'—the latter garments were for
corpses. Gerry was renowned for his belief in de Valera,
and his belief in the contention that cycling made one
mad.

One day, when they were both in their seventies,
Matt wrote inviting Gerry to come and see him—he
had something urgent to convey. He addressed the
letter:

> Gerry O'Brien,
>   c/o Matt O'Brien,
>   The Square,
>   Drumcollogher,
>   Co. Limerick.

The following day the letter came back. On inspec-
tion Matt presumed that it must be an urgent com-
munication for Gerry so he hired Farrell the local
hackney driver, and they both ploughed up to Gerry's
farm.

Matt handed Gerry the letter and the latter, who was
obsessionally secretive, put the letter in his pocket
unopened, while the two discussed the weather, old
times, the drapery trade, farming etc.

Once Matt and the hackney driver had departed, Gerry read the letter. Then he went down to see Matt.

Matt was surprised to see his brother so soon and when Gerry explained by pulling Matt's letter from his pocket, Matt couldn't remember what it was he had written it for in the first place.

Seamus Mallon

DEPUTY LEADER OF THE SDLP

It is a common misconception that the sole aim of
Lambeg drummers is to thunder the fear of God—and
the Queen—into their neighbours as a ritual reminder
of their proper station in life. The discerning are aware,
however, of a select body of performers who stroke the
skins with the sensitivity of a Menehuin. Matt
Copeland was one of these. Not for him the muscular
tom-tom of the 'Twelfth' or 'Black Saturday'—that was
for the potwallopers. He geared himself for the 'Clady'.
This was the connossieur's competition. There was
a £300 prize. Big bets were struck and the winner
wrote himself into local folk-lore.

Matt arrived on my door-step that Friday morning
at eight. The desperation in his eyes matched the fear of
being seen at a Catholic politician's door—especially in
July. 'Are ye for Stormont the day, Big Fella?' I

'Are ye for Stormont the day, Big Fella?'

I returned an assenting nod.

'I want ye to do something for me. Will ye?'

'No problem,' I replied.

'Good! Good!' he guttered. 'I need . . .' His eyes sank
slowly to the ground. 'Look, I've got sixty quid on
myself to win the 'Clady' . . . my drum's burst and I need
a pair of hides for tonight. Will ye get them for me?'

The proud eyes came as near to pleading as ever a
man like Matt could get. Refusing him was out of the
question. Squeezing the address and money into my
hand he made for the gate. Then he stopped, only the

head turned. The grey eyes drilled me.

'If ye haven't them to me by seven they'll disqualify me . . . I'll be skint . . . and . . . and you'll be the t--d they say you are!'

The cap disappeared round the privet.

The only business in Stormont that day was the pre-holiday adjournment debate when members indulge their prejudices untrammelled by time or the rules of serious debate. After a disjointed peroration on the tourist potential of scenic South Armagh the call of the bar was almost irresistable. However Matt's parting shot—and concern for the future well-being of my windows—drove me towards 'Sam McWhirter and Son' of Sandy Row. Crossing the Boyne Bridge into Sandy Row I glanced up at the arches—threating gantries of red, white and blue, extolling me to 'Fear God and Honour the Queen!'. I was not reassured. My relationship with the latter was to say the least strained; with the former, somewhat neglected. A fluttering street banner proclaimed 'Liberty and Brotherhood to all loyal subjects'. Conscious of a distinct deficiency in the one essential virtue, I scuttled into 'McWhirter's'.

Sam, the father, eyed me over the top edge of wire-framed spectacles. We exchanged greetings and conducted our business.

'Would you wrap them up please,' I finished, 'I have to carry them to my car.'

He shook his head resignedly and laughed: 'Do ye know naffin, man. Lambeg hides have to be kept flat and stretched. If ye roll them they're ruined. Help him out with them, Sam!'

Sam, the son, stretched them properly on the back seat of the car.

'Them's great hides,' he confided. 'Them was tuck from a couple of ten year old bucks out at Cullybackey. They'll beat a treat , . .'

I had an hour to meet Matt's deadline. Easy. A satisfying sense of achievement mingled with a growing feeling of magnanimity. I had breached the great cultural divide. Like Paul after Damascus, I felt purged. That the miracle had been wrought not by a shaft of divine light but through the agency of Sam the Father, Sam the Son and two buck goats from Cullybackey in no way diminished the sensation. I reached the outskirts of Portadown.

With my prejudiced past behind me, I felt a wave of confidence as I wound down the window at the checkpoint. I smiled warmly as I addressed the constable. His eyes scanned the inside of the car and then lit up when he saw the hides. The empathy was almost tangible.

'Ah, good man. Them look like right good skins you've got!'

The news that I had just purchased them in Sandy Row noticeably added to the good-will radiating between us.

'Sure we'll not detain you, Sur. Drive on, and the best of luck!'

It was too good to last. His fellow yeoman—face obscured by sidelocks—sprang to the defence of queen and country.

'Hould on a minute. You're Mallon aren't you?' I nodded. 'Out—and put your hands up in the air. What's them hides doing in the back of *your* car?' My new-found philanthrophy was ebbing. I was almost my old self again, but I knew that dignity was my only weapon. I reeled off the story in a voice of great authority and confidently lowered my arms to look at my watch. It was a quarter to seven and I still had eight miles to go. With steely politeness I requested that I be allowed to proceed. No chance!

'You'll have to wait here 'till I get you cleared.' He jumbled 'Alphas' and 'Omegas' and 'Rogers' into the inter-com for a full five minutes before re-emerging: 'Alright, sur, on your way.'

I threw caution to the wind. Having survived Sandy Row, a near-fatal attack of good-will and the attentions of the custodians of the peace I could not fail on the last lap. With the throttle opened full and urged on by the distant brattle of drummers warming up, I made it to the edge of the gathering crowd. Ignoring the startled faces I steered my way through to Matt. Impending dementia gave way to relief as he saw my car.

'What kept you? Have you got them?' There was no point in trying to explain. Those two would never have screened Matt as a revolutionary suspect. Besides, he had the door open and the skins whipped out before I could begin to reply.

'Now get outa here,' he muttered as he moved away, 'some of these fellas . . . well, you're not their favourite.'

Matt's victory was duly and noisily celebrated—so much so that he had to spend the following two days in bed. Matt's recovery marked a radical change in his social habits. For the first time in his fifty-seven years he began to drink in the village's 'papish' pub. A worrying act of disloyalty. This was compounded when it became known that he involved himself in long conspiratorial discussions with 'that Mallon'. Surprise gave way to deep concern. It was generally—and regretfully—agreed that Matt was going the wrong way. He would have to be spoken to. Billy Woolsey undertook to perform the pastoral act. After Matt had downed five rums, he began: 'Maybe it's none of my business, Matt, but what's between you and Mallon?' The moment had been long anticipated and a silence descended on the bar. Matt straightened himself; a smile creased his face.

'What's between me and the Big Fella is goats—two ten year old bucks from Cullybackey. Does that satisfy ye, ye hide-bound eejit.' With that Matt established his independence. His abberation would have to be tolerated.

Two buck goats from Cullybackey and one small leap for mankind!

INDEX